The Fundamentally Simple Logic of Language

D0879607

The Fundamentally Simple Logic of Language: Learning a Second Language with the Tools of the Native Speaker presents a data-driven approach to understanding how native speakers do not use subject and direct object to process language.

Native speakers know who does what by applying intuitively two simple inferences that are argued to be part of universal grammar. The book explains and exemplifies these two inferences throughout. These two inferences explain the native speaker's ease of acquisition and use, and answer difficult questions for linguistics (transitivity, case, semantic roles) in such a way that undergraduate students and second language learners can understand these concepts and apply them to their own language acquisition. While Spanish is used as the primary example, the theory can be applied to many other languages.

This book will appeal to teachers and learners of any second language, as well as linguists interested in second language acquisition, in second language teaching, and in argument structure.

Luis H. González is an associate professor of Spanish and linguistics at Wake Forest University. He completed his Ph.D. at the University of California, Davis. His main areas of research are semantic roles, case, reflexivization, clitic doubling, differential object marking, dichotomies in language, Spanish linguistics, and second language learning. He is the co-author of *Gramática para la composición* (Georgetown UP), a Spanish advanced grammar and writing textbook, now in its third edition (2016). He is also the author of *Cómo entender y cómo enseñar* por *y* para, published by Routledge in 2020, and *Four Dichotomies in Spanish: Adjective Position, Adjectival Clauses, Ser/Estar, and Preterite/Imperfect*, published by Routledge in 2021.

The Fundamentally Simple Logic of Language

Learning a Second Language with the Tools of the Native Speaker

Luis H. González

Routledge
Taylor & Francis Group

LONDON AND NEW YORK

First published 2021
by Routledge
2 Park Square, Milton Park, Abingdon, Oxon OX14 4RN

and by Routledge
52 Vanderbilt Avenue, New York, NY 10017

Routledge is an imprint of the Taylor & Francis Group, an informa business

© 2021 Luis H. González

British Library Cataloguing-in-Publication Data
A catalogue record for this book is available from the British Library .

Library of Congress Cataloging-in-Publication Data
Names: González, Luis H., author.
Title: The fundamentally simple logic of language : learning a second
language with the tools of the native speaker / Luis H. González.
Description: Abingdon, Oxon ; New York, NY : Routledge, 2021. |
Includes bibliographical references and index.
Identifiers: LCCN 2020043445 (print) | LCCN 2020043446 (ebook) |
ISBN 9780367688295 (hardback) | ISBN 9781003139225 (ebook)
Subjects: LCSH: Grammar, Comparative and general--Verb phrase. |
Native language--Study and teaching. | Language and languages--Study and
teaching--Foreign speakers. | Second language acquisition.
Classification: LCC P281 .G66 2021 (print) | LCC P281 (ebook) |
DDC 418.0071--dc23
LC record available at https://lccn.loc.gov/2020043445
LC ebook record available at https://lccn.loc.gov/2020043446

ISBN: 978-0-367-68829-5 (hbk)
ISBN: 978-0-367-68831-8 (pbk)
ISBN: 978-1-003-13922-5 (ebk)

Typeset in Times New Roman
by Deanta Global Publishing Services, Chennai, India

To those whose teaching makes a difference in the lives of their learners; to those who learn to make a difference in their community, both near and far.

Contents

Tables

Acknowledgments

This book began to come together a good few years ago. I presented on semantic roles at The University of North Carolina at Chapel Hill in the Linguistics Colloquium in 1998. Ivan Sag was the keynote speaker. After my presentation, he graciously said, "everything that you said against semantic roles as we understand them now is true". I will never forget that moment. Those lucky enough to have known Ivan will understand why I am recognizing him first. I had a few minutes with him that evening at a dinner at Gert Webelhut's home. Ivan's encouraging words will stay with me forever. Tears came to my eyes several times after I read about his passing. Ivan made a difference in the lives of his students in a way that few teachers do. Many of those students did not take a class with him.

Bob Hemmer told me, also at The University of North Carolina at Chapel Hill, more than twenty years ago: "I wish I had studied with a grammar like this when I was learning Spanish". He also told me five years ago, "I have not read anything this creative in a long time". He encouraged me to find the right home for this manuscript. That home is Routledge. Many heart-felt thanks to my wonderful editor, Samantha Vale Noya, and to her wonderful editorial assistant, Rosie McEwan. They helped in unknown ways in the efforts to publish this project. Now that this dream has been accomplished, another dream is to meet in person and celebrate this book, a couple of other ones already published, and perhaps a couple more in the future. Wouldn't that be sweet? Both, meeting in person and a couple more books.

My colleagues of the Linguistics Circle at Wake Forest University have provided feedback over the years when my students or I have presented parts of this work. I will not mention names so I do not forget any important one. Thanks to those who read chapters or provided examples, double-checked them, or answered questions about their language: Servio Becerra, Tina Boyer, Diego Burgos, Peter Floyd, Mary Friedman, Ola Furmanek, Judy Kem, Hosun Kim, Matt Mayers, Gabriel Quiroz, Yasuko Takata Rallings, Rob Ulery, Stan Whitley, Nick Wolters. Silvia Tiboni-Craft and Jessie Craft deserve special thanks for their help with Italian and Latin. Thanks also to Jim Mitchnowicz for starting Slinki (Spanish linguistics in the Carolinas) and to Rebecca Ronquest for coming onboard and helping Jim nurture it. Some of this work has been presented at Slinki by my students and by me. Thanks to all the Slinkiers.

Many students over the years have provided comments or done research with me. Two undergraduates in their first year in college provided detailed comments for every chapter and answered many questions: Kyle Cattin and Audrey Dyer. They are the two angels of TFSLL. Chicago Power! Other students who provided feedback and listened to me (sometimes for hours) are Maddie Barnes, Allie Blum, Meghan Bredbenner, Marisa Busquets, Kingsley Bustamante, Michael Davern, Katie Dickens (the stitcher), Brandon Freeman, Devin Gilbert, Anna Grace Guercio, Kristin Johnson, Trey Kieser, Austin Moore, Sapna Pathak, Harsh Patolia, Angela Pegarella, Marianna Pipino, Chelsea Privette, Emma Rogers, Mary Catherine Rich, Ana Paola Rubio, Savarni Sanka, Leah Shoup, Allie Silverglate, Coby Schneider, Peter Till, Peter Wallace, Ann Wheat (aka Annie Sweet). Annie was the first student to provide detailed comments on the first versions of several chapters. *¡Muchísimas gracias!* to all of you, and to many whom I undoubtedly forgot to mention here. You know that you have a place in my heart. Among them, Cristina, Jason, and Josh, whose last names I do not remember now. But I remember the sparkle in the eye and the laughter.

Finally, thanks to Ana, Sara, and Andres for all of their patience. There might be a couple more books. Hopefully, those books will be the ones waiting this time. Thanks also to Roberto Luis for seeing the dream like nobody else has seen it yet.

Peter Wallace, an undergraduate student, wrote to me one day in 2018, "Professor, this is the fundamentally simple logic of language". Those words ended as the title. How about that!

Luis H. González
Wake Forest University, September 3, 2020

1 How subject, direct object, and indirect object really work

1.1. Introduction   *Verber vs Verbed*

It is paradoxical that children understand and use subject, direct object, and indirect object in their native language by age seven, yet learning these distinctions in a second language (L2) is so challenging that even scholars cannot agree on whether a certain object is direct or indirect. *Roberto* and *taxes* are the subject in *Roberto worked* and *taxes increased*, yet *Roberto* did something, but *taxes* are really an underlying direct object (taxes were increased). This book shows evidence from Spanish, Italian, and English that applying a VERBER INFERENCE and a VERBED INFERENCE drawn from any sentence is how speakers know who/what is the subject and direct object. If it is true that *the government increased taxes*, it is also true that *the government* is the INCREASER (and *the government* is the subject). That is the verber inference. It is also true that *taxes* were (the) INCREASED. That is the verbed inference (and *taxes* is the direct object). The use of these two simple inferences explains the ease of acquisition of one's native language (L1) and why using subject and direct object to teach languages is not optimal. By using the verber and verbed inferences, learning a second language (L2) will be more like learning your first language and less like learning a foreign language. The verber and the verbed inferences are the heart of *the fundamentally simple logic of language,* a phrase that one of my students used to refer to the explanations proposed in this book for how language works.

This book shows that the GRAMMATICAL RELATIONS subject, direct object, and indirect object are not optimal tools to study and teach languages. Those notions go back to the first grammars of Greek, in which it was proposed that the subject is marked with the NOMINATIVE CASE, the case (the form) of *he* in *he gave her a book*. The **direct object** is marked with the ACCUSATIVE CASE, the case of *he* in *she loved **him***. The indirect object is marked with the DATIVE CASE, the case of *to her* in *he gave a book to her*.[1]

This book also allows teachers of language (and college and high school students) to understand language concepts that are currently understood only by linguists. Most of the specialized terms that the reader must understand have already been covered in the preceding paragraphs. In order to keep the exposition as reader friendly as possible, theoretical references have been kept to a minimum. Instead, due credit will be given, and key theoretical concepts will be briefly explained in Chapter 6. There are a few places where credit must be given, and where references to current theories are unavoidable. But those references are kept to a minimum, and they are explained as clearly as possible, and duly exemplified.

The verber and the verbed inferences reduce the five subject properties and five direct object properties that speakers presumably use to determine subject and direct object in a sentence, as proposed in Dowty (1991: 576), to only two properties (see §6.2). As you read this chapter, <u>you are the reader</u> and **the chapter is the read**. As explained in the first paragraph, <u>verber</u> and **verbed** show a difference in function between *Roberto* and *taxes* that the notion of subject has blurred for 22 centuries, since nominative, accusative, and dative (and other cases) were proposed in Greek.

This chapter is organized as follows. §1.2 shows how speakers can distinguish subject from direct object in their language, without any instruction. §1.3 shows how to distinguish direct object from indirect object. §1.4 shows how to distinguish direct from indirect object when the sentence has a double object. English is a double object language. §1.5 offers some conclusions.

1.2. <u>The verber is always the subject, but the subject is not always the verber</u>

Consider these simple sentences:

(1) a. <u>Julio</u> taught **Spanish**.
    b. <u>Julio</u> sent **an email**.
    c. <u>Julio</u> wrote **a recommendation**.
    d. <u>Julio</u> gave **a book** (to you).

If we want to determine who/what the <u>teacher</u>, the <u>sender</u>, the <u>writer</u>, and the <u>giver</u> is, there is total agreement that it is <u>Julio</u>. If we want to determine who/what the **taught**, the **sent**, the **written**, or the **given** (gift) is, there is total agreement that *Spanish is the taught, an email the sent, a recommendation the written*, and *a book the given* (gift).

Consider the passive voice versions of the sentences in (1):

(2) a. **Spanish** was taught (by Julio).
     b. **An email** was sent (by Julio).
     c. **A recommendation** was written (by Julio).
     d. **A book** was given (by Julio).

Although relatively few speakers of a given language know explicitly what passive voice is, all speakers of a language with passive voice use it, as your familiarity with (2a-d) shows. Speakers of English know *implicitly* that if the sentences in (1) are true, all of the sentences in (2) are true as well, because the sentences in (2) are INFERENCES from the sentences in (1).

What is an inference? If it is true that Julio taught Spanish, sent an email, wrote a recommendation, and gave a book, it is also true that:

(3) a. **Spanish** was (the) taught.
     b. **An email** was (the) sent.
     c. **A recommendation** was (the) written.
     d. **A book** was (the) given.

All of the sentences in (2) and (3) are ENTAILMENTS or INFERENCES. We will use the term *inference* because it is more intuitive and transparent than entailment. An INFERENCE is a logical consequence of a premise or set of premises. In plain English, an inference is a sentence that follows logically from another sentence: if it is true that Julio taught Spanish, it is also true that Julio was the teacher, that Spanish was taught by Julio, and that Spanish was (the) taught. Conversely, it is neither true that Julio was the taught nor is it true that Spanish was the teacher. Of course, Julio is also the sender, writer, and giver, and an email the sent, a recommendation the written, and a book the given. The observation that passive voice is an *inference* is crucial to understanding how subject, direct object, and indirect object really work, which is one of the main goals of this book.

This chapter shows that two simple inferences (Julio is the teacher and Spanish was the taught) are the tools that speakers use to distinguish subject and direct object, and these two inferences explain the choice of subject and direct object in any sentence, a choice for which no linguistic theory has provided a satisfactory explanation until now. The following quote from Dowty (1991: 581) shows the difficulties to distinguish subject from direct object:

> There is in fact one relatively small group of verbs, including *receive, inherit, come into (an inheritance), undergo, sustain (an injury), suffer (from), submit to, succumb to* and *tolerate*, which seem to have

Goals (*receive*, etc.) or Patients (*undergo*, etc.) as subjects, but Agents or causes as other arguments. Perhaps the appropriate comment is that these are in fact exceptions; but they are few in number, so the selection principle is not an absolute rule but is nevertheless a strong tendency.

The verber and verbed inferences account for all of these exceptions (and many others brought up by scholars working on this issue), as this book will show.[2]

We will call the inference that shows the function of <u>Julio</u> in (1a-d) the <u>VERBER INFERENCE</u> and the inference that shows the function of **Spanish, an email, a recommendation**, and **a book** the **VERBED INFERENCE**. Those two simple inferences show how subject and direct object really work.

(4) a. <u>Julio</u> taught **Spanish**.
     b. <u>Julio</u> is <u>the teacher</u>.   (The verber inference)
     c. **Spanish** is **the taught**.   (The verbed inference)
     d. #<u>Julio</u> is **the taught**.[3]   (The verbed inference)
     e. #**Spanish** is the <u>teacher</u>.   (The verber inference)

Thus, *Julio* passes the <u>verber</u> inference (and does not pass the **verbed** inference), and the opposite is true for *Spanish*. The reader can apply these two inferences to sentences (1b-d). Since (1a-d) are all transitive (each has subject and direct object), we have shown so far that the verber is the subject and the verbed is the direct object.

Let us introduce a simple complication in (5a,b), two intransitive sentences:

(5) a. Julio worked.
     b. Taxes increased.

Let us apply the verber inference and the verbed inference to them:

(6) a. <u>Julio</u> worked.
     b. <u>Julio</u> is <u>the worker</u>.   (The verber inference)
     c. #<u>Julio</u> is the worked.   (cf. #the worked Julio)
(7) a. **Taxes** increased.
     b. #**Taxes** are the increaser.
     c. **Taxes** are the **increased**.   (The verbed inference)

Thus, *Julio* passes the verber inference, as (7b) shows; *taxes* pass the verbed inference, as (7c) shows. That means that *Julio* is the verber but *taxes* are the verbed, although both are the subject of (5a,b).

Sentences (1a-d) are similar in that each has verber and verbed. On the other hand, are the sentences in (5a,b) rather similar or rather different? They are similar in the sense that each has a subject and a verb. They are different in the sense that in (5a) the subject is the <u>verber</u> (*Julio*), but in (5b) the subject is the **verbed** (*taxes*). The surface similarity masks a deep difference. Therefore, <u>verber</u> and **verbed** are not another label for subject and direct object because the verber is always the subject of the sentence, but the verbed can be the direct object (as in 1a-d), but it can also be the subject (as in 2a-d and 5b).

In linguistics, the discovery that the subject of sentences similar to (5b) is an underlying direct object is called the Unaccusative Hypothesis (UH), and David Perlmutter is credited with developing it. Perlmutter (1978: 185) states that, "The Unaccusative Hypothesis developed itself in joint work with Paul Postal".

<u>Verber</u> and **verbed** are terms that this writer proposed in his dissertation (González 1997). Those terms originated in semantic roles, an idea proposed in linguistics in 1965 by Jeffrey Gruber (published as Gruber 1976). Levin & Rappaport Hovav (2005) and Williams (2015) are very complete discussions of semantic roles over the last 55 years.

The <u>verber</u> and **verbed** inferences have been tested for over twenty years. The discovery of this difference leads to the observation that the notion of subject has obscured the difference between the sentences in (5a,b) – and countless other sentences with just a subject – for over 22 centuries. We will show later that this distinction explains the ease of acquisition of the native language, something that children accomplish without any instruction by age seven (Snyder & Hyams 2015).

With our understanding of verber and verbed so far, we can now propose a principle of how speakers determine who or what is the subject and the direct object in a sentence. This principle is modeled after the most invoked theory of ARGUMENT selection in linguistics, that of Dowty (1991). Roughly speaking, *argument* is a specialized word in linguistics for each mandatory participant in a sentence, depending on the verb. Therefore, ARGUMENT STRUCTURE (or ARGUMENT REALIZATION, as Levin & Rappaport Hovav called their 2005 book) is a theory of how speakers distinguish subject from direct object (and indirect object).

(8)   Verber/Verbed Argument Selection Principle (VVASP)

> The participant in a sentence that passes the verber inference is expressed as the subject; the participant that passes the verbed inference is expressed as the direct object of a transitive sentence, but as the subject of an intransitive or an intransitivized one.

Now we can provide a definition of transitivity in terms of <u>verber</u> and **verbed**:

(9)   <u>Verber</u>/**Verbed** definition of transitivity:

> A sentence is transitive if and only if it has a <u>verber</u> AND a **verbed**. A sentence is intransitive if and only if it has a <u>verber</u> OR a **verbed**, but not both.

The sentences in (1) are all transitive because they all have a <u>verber</u> and a **verbed**. The ones in (2) and (5b) are INTRANSITIVIZED because they have only a **verbed**. The one in (5a) is intransitive. Readers know now that the subject of each of the passive voice sentences in (2) is a **verbed**.

An INTRANSITIVIZED sentence is a variation of a transitive sentence whose <u>verber</u> or **verbed** has been omitted. An INTRANSITIVE sentence is a sentence that never has a <u>verber</u> and a **verbed**. It has one or the other, but never both. Thus, (5b) is intransitivized but (5a) is intransitive. We will see that there are verberless sentences, but there are not subjectless ones.

To summarize, in a sentence without a preposition, the participant that passes the <u>verber</u> inference is always the subject and the one that passes the **verbed** inference is the direct object, but the subject if there is no <u>verber</u>. A transitive sentence has <u>verber</u> and **verbed**. If there is a <u>verber</u>, it is always the subject. However, the **verbed** is always the direct object of a transitive sentence but the subject of a verberless one. Passive voice sentences (like those in 2a-d) are verberless but not subjectless. In the absence of a <u>verber</u>, the **verbed** is expressed as the subject. The notion of subject has blurred, until now, the observation that many subjects are really the **verbed**; that is, an underlying direct object that was promoted to subject.

Exercise 1. Determine who or what the VERBER is and who or what the VERBED is for each sentence.

Ex: Miriam studies law.
Verber: <u>Miriam</u>; verbed: <u>law</u>.

1/2. Gabriel balanced his checkbook.
Verber: _Gabriel_ ; verbed: _checkbook_

3/4. The surgeon removed the tumor.
Verber: _Surgeon_ ; verbed: _tumor_

5/6. The fire destroyed the garage.
Verber: _fire_ ; verbed: _garage_

7/8. Aunt Rose remodeled the garage.
Verber: _Aunt Rose_ ; verbed: _garage_

9/10. The painting astonished the tourists.
Verber: _painting_ ; verbed: _tourists_

11/12. The tourists admired the painting.
Verber: _tourists_ ; verbed: _painting_

13/14. This device monitors blood pressure.
Verber: _device_ ; verbed: _blood pressure_

15/16. My hand touched the buckle.
Verber: _hand_ ; verbed: _buckle_

17/18. The buckle touched my hand.
Verber: _buckle_ ; verbed: _hand_

19/20. This article will open doors.
Verber: _article_ ; verbed: _doors_

21/22. H and O make up water.
Verber: _H2O_ ; verbed: _water_

23/24. Uncle George underwent heart surgery.
Verber: _Uncle George_ ; verbed: _heart surgery_

25/26. The river moved those stones.
Verber: _river_ ; verbed: _stones_

27/28. Rosa fears horror movies.
Verber: _Rosa_ ; verbed: _horror movies_

29/30. Horror movies frighten Rosa.
Verber: _Horror movies_; verbed: _Rosa_

Answers. The subject is always the verber in these sentences and the other participant is the verbed. At first sight, this exercise seems trivial in English. However, observe 21/22. How do we know that speakers of English say that *H and O make up water* but not that *Water makes up H and O*? Thanks to the verbed inference. Any speaker will admit that the sentence *water is made up of H and O* makes sense. On the other hand, any reader will realize that the sentence *H and O are made up of water* does not make sense, and nobody says that.

Observe also 23/24. Is Uncle George the agent or the cause? Uncle George satisfies more properties of a "patient". In several linguistic theories, Uncle George should be the direct object. Suffice it to say that speakers of English never say *heart surgery underwent Uncle George*. Determining subject and direct object is *not* trivial for one third of these sentences in many other languages. However, once speakers are aware of the verber and verbed inferences, that decision becomes easier. Sentences 27/28 and 29/30 will be discussed in detail in Chapters 3–5, in both Spanish and English. Several of these sentences (or similar ones) will be discussed throughout this book, particularly in Chapter 6.

Exercise 2. All of the sentences in Exercise 1 are transitive; that is, they have <u>verber</u> and **verbed**. The following sentences are intransitive or intransitivized; that is, they have either <u>verber</u> or **verbed**, but not both. Determine whether the single participant is the <u>verber</u> or the <u>verbed</u>. Write two dashes in the other space. Answers after the exercise.

Ex: Birds fly.
Verber: <u>birds</u> ; verbed: --

Ex: Prices increased.
Verber: -- ; verbed: <u>prices</u>

31/32. Margarita was born yesterday.
Verber: ; verbed:

33/34. Spiders bite.
Verber: ; verbed:

35/36. Clouds appeared.
Verber: _____; verbed: _____

37/38. The mail arrived.
Verber: _____; verbed: _____

39/40. Manuela studied in Medellín.
Verber: _____; verbed: _____

41/42. Our team won.
Verber: _____; verbed: _____

43/44. The discussion finished.
Verber: _____; verbed: _____

Answers: Verbers: spiders, Manuela, our team. All of the other participants are the verbed.

1.3. Distinguishing the direct object from the indirect object

Let us assume that the indirect object is the beneficiary (or the maleficiary)
in a sentence. That is actually true because the intuition behind indirect
object originated as the participant who receives the gift (Butt 2006: 13).
Readers can now determine who is the <u>verber</u>, **verbed**, and beneficiary
in (10):

(10) a. Julio taught Spanish to you.
     b. Julio sent an email to you.
     c. Julio wrote a recommendation for you.
     d. Julio gave a book to you.

Readers already know how to distinguish <u>verber</u> and **verbed**. The other participant is, of course, the beneficiary. Let us now introduce a complication.
We will express the sentences in (10) as those in (11), which are called in
English *the dative shift alternation* or *the double object alternation* of the
sentences in (10):[4]

(11) a. Julio taught you Spanish.
     b. Julio sent you an email.
     c. Julio wrote you a recommendation.
     d. Julio gave you a book.

Apparently, there is no indirect object in the sentences in (11) because the intuition behind the indirect object is that it is "mediated" by a preposition, and not directly "governed" by the verb. In English, that preposition is either *to* (as in 10a,b,d) or *for* (as in 10c). In English linguistics, instead of a direct and an indirect object as in (10a-d), we have in (11a-d) a PRIMARY object (you) and a SECONDARY object (Dryer 1986: 814). Is *you* still the beneficiary in (11a-d) or not? There is absolutely no doubt that Julio is the verber. We also know who or what is the **verbed** in (10a-d). The crucial question is: is the **verbed** in each of the sentences in (11) the same as in each of those in (10), regardless of the change in word order and the omission of the preposition (*to* or *for*)? Is there a difference in meaning, as some linguists claim?[5]

Readers can answer the preceding questions after considering sentence (12a) and the syntactic alternations (variations) in (12b-d):

(12) a.   The Academy gave **an Oscar** to Sandra Bullock.
   b.   The Academy gave Sandra Bullock **an Oscar**. (Dative-shift sentence)
   c.   **An Oscar** was given to Sandra Bullock (by The Academy). (Passive voice)
   d.   Sandra Bullock was given **an Oscar** (by The Academy). (Passive voice of the indirect object)

If readers have to determine subject, direct object, and indirect object for (12a-d), the task is somewhat of a puzzle: *The Academy* is the subject in (12a,b) but a "by phrase" in (12c,d), and it can even be left out, as the parentheses in (12c,d) indicate. *An Oscar* is the direct object in (12a,d); the secondary object in (12b); and the subject in (12c). Sandra Bullock is the indirect object in (12a,c); the primary object in (12b); and the subject in (12d). We will see that with verber and verbed, there is no need to distinguish the "primary" object from the "secondary" object. Furthermore, the reader has just noticed how subject, direct object, and indirect object vary greatly in position in (12a-d).

On the other hand, if the reader has to determine who the giver, the given, and the beneficiary are for (12a), the answers are uncontroversial: The Academy is the giver, an Oscar the given, and Sandra Bullock the beneficiary. What about (12b-d)? The giver, the given, and the beneficiary are CONSTANT, regardless of each participant being expressed as the subject, the direct object, the indirect object, a primary object, or a secondary object.[6] Thus, whereas verber, verbed, and beneficiary are constant in different variations of a sentence *with the same meaning*, subject, direct object, and indirect object are VARIABLE. Surprisingly, the teaching of languages has been based on three concepts that vary in common variations of many sentences. And this has been happening since the notion of subject, direct object, and indirect object were proposed approximately 22 centuries ago by the first Greek grammarians. The observation that we have been teaching languages with variables explains part of the difficulty of learning an L2. The ease of acquisition of one's native language suggests that native speakers are using verber and verbed.

Now we all can agree on the answers for the sentences in (11): *you* is the beneficiary in (11), as is *you* in (10). Even when we say in English that someone was taught or told **something**, we understand that a teacher taught or told **something** to that person. It is even clearer that if Julio sent you **an email** or gave you **a book**, he did not send you anywhere nor did he give you to anyone. He sent or gave you **something**, and you are the beneficiary.

1.4. Verber, verbed, and beneficiary

Distinguishing verber from **verbed** is easier than distinguishing subject from direct object. In fact, if we can distinguish verber from **verbed**, the third participant is a beneficiary, as we determined in (11). You can test your understanding so far with (13):

(13) We sent Grandma our children.

It is uncontroversial who the sender is. Who is the sent and who is the beneficiary? Depending on who is doing what, either *they* or *she* will be doing some traveling, and *they* and *she* are at our children's house or at Grandma's house. One of them is the sent. The other is the beneficiary (they/she will "get" someone). Is it clear who is the sent and who is the beneficiary? Did we send *our children* or did we send *Grandma*? If there is any doubt, let us "unshift" (13) as in (14):

(14) We sent our children to Grandma.

It is uncontroversial who the sender, the sent, and the beneficiary are, and they are the same as in (13).

Exercise 3. Determine who or what is the verber, who or what is the verbed, and who or what is the beneficiary/maleficiary in each of the following sentences.

45–47. The Academy gave an Oscar to Sandra Bullock.
Verber: _____; verbed: _____; beneficiary/maleficiary: _____

48–50. The Academy gave Sandra Bullock an Oscar.
Verber: _____; verbed: _____; beneficiary/maleficiary: _____

51–53. Sandra Bullock was given an Oscar.
Verber: _____; verbed: _____; beneficiary/maleficiary: _____

54–56. I sent Mara Boston a book to Boston.
Verber: _____; verbed: _____; beneficiary/maleficiary: _____

57–59. We sent Grandma our children.
Verber: _____; verbed: _____; beneficiary/maleficiary: _____

60–62. Small fonts give me a headache.
Verber: _____; verbed: _____; beneficiary/maleficiary: _____

63–65. This jerk gave me the finger.
Verber: _____; verbed: _____; beneficiary/maleficiary: _____

66–68. Give me a break!
Verber: _____; verbed: _____; beneficiary/maleficiary: _____

(Chapter 4 discusses some of these examples in detail).

Answers to exercise 3

45–47. <u>The Academy</u> gave **an Oscar** <u>to Sandra Bullock</u>.

48–50. <u>The Academy</u> gave <u>Sandra Bullock</u> **an Oscar**.

51–53. <u>Sandra Bullock</u> was given **an Oscar**.

54–56. <u>I</u> sent <u>Mara Boston</u> **a book** to Boston.

57–59. <u>We</u> sent <u>Grandma</u> **our children**.

60–62. <u>Small fonts</u> give <u>me</u> **a headache**.

63–65. <u>This jerk</u> gave <u>me</u> **the finger**.

66–68. (<u>You</u>) Give <u>me</u> **a break**!

1.5. Conclusions

How do we distinguish subject from direct object, and more importantly, a direct object from an indirect object? It is rather difficult. Is *Roberto* similar to *taxes* in *Roberto worked* and *Taxes increased*? They are similar in FORM, since both are the subject of the corresponding sentence. Regarding MEANING, they are clearly different. How do we distinguish verber, verbed, and beneficiary? It is very clear. The verber passes the verber inference and it is invariably the subject of a sentence in the active voice. The verbed passes the verbed inference and it is the direct object of a transitive sentence or the subject of a sentence without a verber. The indirect object is the beneficiary or maleficiary. In a sentence with a double object in English (13), the beneficiary is always the primary object: it is always preceding the secondary object, it is the only one of the two objects that can "unshift", and it is overwhelmingly human. When the primary object unshifts, it will always require the preposition *to* or *for*. This is an unequivocal way of determining who is doing what to whom in a sentence, which is the heart of language understanding and production. If a learner of a language is not clear as to who is doing what to whom, misunderstanding will undoubtedly happen.[7]

There is a built-in simplification for linguistic theory in this explanation. If the beneficiary or maleficiary can be easily distinguished from the **verbed** (it is invariably the primary object, it never passes the **verbed** inference, it is overwhelmingly more animate than the verbed, and it will take *to* or *for* when unshifted), then the task of argument structure is simply distinguishing verber from **verbed**. That is a simplification of one third in sheer number, without factoring in the level of complexity (the difficulty to tell apart direct objects from indirect objects) that is "erased". In Spanish, the difference between direct and indirect object is as blurry as that between the subject of sentences like *Roberto worked* and *Taxes increased.*

The observation that children acquire passive voice between the ages of three and seven (basically, the verbed inference) allows the prediction that children will be able to tell apart direct object from beneficiary in a second language soon after they can read. This observation invites the hypothesis that some of the concepts discussed in this book will be understood by elementary school children who will be learning an L2. That is a very provocative proposition –ambiguity intended – for research and for L2 learning.

Notes

1 The verber is underlined; the **verbed** is in bold, and the beneficiary is double underlined.

2 Chapter 6 will briefly discuss Dowty (1991) and a few other theories on how speakers determine who is the subject and the direct object in a sentence.

3 The notation '#' means that the sentence is not a logical inference (it does not follow) from the sentence at issue. This notation comes from Huddleston and Pullum (2002: 35). They use the more specialized term *entailment*.

4 The dative (the indirect object) shifts places with the accusative (the direct object). The preposition that introduces the indirect object (*to* or *for* in English) must be omitted. Now the sentence has two "direct" objects instead of one direct and one indirect ("indirectly" governed by the verb through a preposition).

5 Portero Muñoz (2003: 140), Van Valin & LaPolla (1997: 336), Van Valin (2004), among others. These Role and Reference Grammar analyses claim that the PP becomes an undergoer in the double object construction. They also claim that the students learned French when *someone taught the students French*, but that they might not have learned when *someone taught French to the students*. The passivization of a dative object in the language might be misleading linguists coming from English. The students are the beneficiaries in both alternations. Would there be a difference in *I told a story to you* vs. *I told you a story* or in *my wife gave a kiss to me* and *my wife gave me a kiss*?

6 With verber and verbed, there is no need for the distinction between *primary* and *secondary* object.

7 The question whether an object is direct or indirect is even harder to answer for languages that still maintain a difference in direct and indirect object pronouns. Chapters 3 to 5 will discuss that issue in detail for English and Spanish.

References

Butt, Miriam. 2006. *Theories of case*. New York: Cambridge University Press.

Dowty, David. 1991. Thematic proto-roles and argument selection. *Language* 67. 547–619. (https://www.jstor.org/stable/pdf/415037).

Dryer, Mathew S. 1986. Primary objects, secondary objects, and antidative. *Language* 62. 808–845. (https://www.jstor.org/stable/pdf/415173).

González, Luis H. 1997. *Transitivity and structural case marking in psych verbs. An HPSG fragment of a grammar of Spanish*. Davis: University of California. (Doctoral dissertation.)

Gruber, Jeffrey S. 1976. *Lexical structures in syntax and semantics*. Amsterdam: North-Holland.

Huddleston, Rodney & Pullum, Geoffrey K. 2002. *The Cambridge grammar of the English language*. Cambridge: Cambridge University Press.

Levin, Beth & Rappaport Hovav, Malka. 2005. *Argument realization*. Cambridge: Cambridge University Press.

Perlmutter, David M. 1978. Impersonal passives and the unaccusative hypothesis. *BLS* 4. 157–189. https://doi.org/10.3765/bls.v4i0.2198.

Portero Muñoz, Carmen. 2003. Derived nominalizations in –ee: A role and reference grammar based semantic analysis. *English Language and Linguistics* 7(1). 129–159. https://doi.org/10.1017/S1360674303211059.

Snyder, William & Hyams, Nina. 2015. Minimality effects in children's passives. In Di Domenico, Elisa & Hamann, Cornelia & Matteini, Simona (eds.), *Structures, strategies and beyond: Essays in honour of Adriana Belletti*, 343–368. (*Linguistik Aktuell/Linguistics Today 223*). Amsterdam/Philadelphia: John Benjamins. https://doi.org/10.1075/la.223.16sny.

Van Valin, Robert D., Jr. 2004. Semantic macroroles in role and reference grammar. In Kailuweit, Rolf & Hummel, Martin (eds.), *Semantische Rollen*, 62–82. Tübingen: Gunter Narr Verlag. (http://www.acsu.buffalo.edu/~rrgpage/rrg/vanvalin_papers/Sem_Macroroles_&_Lang_Processing.pdf).

Van Valin, Robert D., Jr. & Lapolla, Randy J. 1997. *Syntax: Structure, meaning and function*. Cambridge: Cambridge University Press.

Williams, Alexander. 2015. *Arguments in syntax and semantics*. Cambridge: Cambridge University Press. (Key topics in syntax). https://doi.org/10.1017/CBO9781139042864.

2 Perfect auxiliary selection using verber and verbed

↳ I am so confused.

2.1. Introduction

This chapter shows that verber and verbed offer a simple explanation for perfect auxiliary choice between *avere/essere* 'have'/'be' in Italian (and languages with a similar choice of auxiliary). A corollary of the explanation accounts for past participle agreement with the subject, when it is required. Section 2 offers evidence from Spanish that the subject of a passive voice sentence and that of a reflexive sentence is the **verbed**; therefore, the reflexive pronoun does not replace the direct object; it replaces the <u>verber</u>. Sections 3 and 4 show evidence from Italian and English that sometimes the subject is an underlying ("original") <u>beneficiary</u> (or <u>maleficiary</u>); that is, an underlying indirect object, the same way that the subject is often an underlying **verbed**. It also explains why reflexive sentences in Italian take *essere*, and why the past participle agrees with the subject when the auxiliary is *essere*.

2.2. Verber, verbed, and beneficiary in languages with a *have/be* distinction

Danish, Dutch, French, and Italian are among several languages with a choice of auxiliary for the perfect tenses (have + PAST PARTICIPLE). Let us exemplify with Italian.

> PAST PARTICIPLE: The form of the verb that follows the auxiliary *have* or *be* in English: *improved* in *my Italian has improved* or *published* in *this book was published in 2021.*

Suppose we are teachers of Italian. We teach our students that if a preverbal participant passes the <u>verber</u> inference, the sentence requires the auxiliary *avere* 'have'. That is true for any transitive sentence (one with verber and **verbed**, like 1a-d in Chapter 1). It is also true for any intransitive sentence whose only participant is the verber (like 5a in Chapter 1). However, if no participant passes the verber inference (as 5b in Chapter 1), the auxiliary in Italian would be *essere* 'be'. This rule is succinctly stated in (7) below.

The typical explanation for *avere*/*essere* 'have'/'be' in most textbooks of French and Italian is that transitive verbs take *avere*. Some intransitive verbs also take *avere*. Other intransitive verbs take *essere*, as shown in textbooks in the famous diagram of the "*casa dell'essere*" or "*maison d'être*" (a few intransitive verbs and verbs of movement in a house, where people can *arrive, come in, enter, go, go up, go/come down, fall* [and *die*], *leave*, etc.). Sentences with a reflexive pronoun also take *essere*, but no explanation is given. Furthermore, the past participle agrees with the subject when the auxiliary is *essere* and when there is a reflexive pronoun in the sentence. The "rules" just mentioned lack a unifying thread. Verber and **verbed** not only improve that explanation; they give L2 learners in college (and perhaps in high school) an understanding of auxiliary selection reserved until now for linguists with a good understanding of the Unaccusative Hypothesis (UH). Remember that the UH is the discovery that the only participant of many sentences is the verbed, not the verber.

Let us now throw a mild complication at our students. The following sentences are based on one from Rosen (1984: 45). With some verbs, either the verber or the **verbed** can be omitted. The prediction of our rule in (7) below is that the auxiliary will be different, depending on which of the two (the verber or the **verbed**) is now the only participant in the sentence. The ungrammatical sentences have not been marked, so readers with some familiarity with Italian (or languages that work like it) can see the point to be made. (Answers will be provided below).[1] In fact, even readers who do not know any Italian can complete this "assignment".

(1) a. Ugo continuò la lotta.
'Ugo continued the battle'.
   b. Ugo ha continuato.
'Ugo has continued'
   c. Ugo è continuato.
'Ugo has continued'
   d. La lotta ha continuato.
'The battle has continued'.
   e. La lotta è continuata.
'The battle has continued'.

Thus, we have four hypothetical intransitivized sentences, but only two are correct. Which are the two correct ones? How do learners know? They simply apply the <u>verber</u> and the **verbed** inferences. The correct sentences are, of course, (1b) and (1e). This explanation comes with a nice bonus: agreement. There appears to be "agreement" in (1b). Is it because *continuato* agrees with Ugo? Or is it because if the auxiliary is *avere*, there is no agreement; that is, the past participle is invariable? We can answer this question by using Francesca instead of Ugo.

(2) a. Francesca continuò la lotta.
         'Francesca continued the battle'.
     b. Francesca ha continuato.
     c. Francesca è continuata.
     d. La lotta ha continuato.
     e. La lotta è continuata.

There is no agreement with *avere* precisely because the preverbal participant is the <u>verber</u>. However, when the preverbal participant is not the <u>verber</u>, the past participle agrees with it. That fact is not "visible" in (1b) vis-à-vis (1c), but it is in (2b) vis-à-vis (2c). As predicted, there is agreement in (1e) and (2e). The grammatical sentences are *Ugo ha continuato, Francesca ha continuato, la lotta è continuata*. Of course, (1a) and (2a) are also grammatical. It is not easy to overstate the importance of students realizing why *Ugo* and *Francesca* take *avere* when there is no **verbed** in the sentence, as in (1b) and (2b), but *la lotta* takes *essere* in (1e) and (2e).

   Let us raise the bar and throw another complication in §2.4 to those students of Italian. But readers will understand section §2.4 better after §2.3.

2.3. Further evidence for a subject that is the verbed

It is uncontroversial that the preverbal participant of a sentence in the passive voice is the **verbed**.[2] That is precisely the point of passivization: expressing the underlying direct object as the subject. Since there is no longer a verber in passive voice sentences, they are intransitive, as per (9) in Chapter 1. Or better yet, they are INTRANSITIVIZED. In addition to passive-voice morphology (was renovated), as in (3b) below, the reflexive pronoun is also an intransitivizing particle in Spanish (and in other languages), as (3c) shows:

(3) a. <u>La decana</u>   renovó   **este edificio.**
         The dean-fem renovated this building
         'The dean renovated this building'.

b. **Este edificio** fue renovado por la decana.
   'This building was renovated by the dean'.

c **Este edificio** <u>se</u>   renovó.
   this building itself renovated
   'This building was renovated'.

d. #<u>La decana</u>   **se**   renovó.
   The dean-fem herself renovated
   'The dean renovated herself'.

e. *Este edificio renovó.
   '*This building renovated'.

If reflexivization were replacement of the direct object (or the indirect object) with a reflexive pronoun, as believed in Spanish grammar (and in the grammar of many other languages), sentence (3d) would be true if (3a) is true.[3] (3d) is not true. If reflexivization is replacement of the <u>verber</u> with a reflexive pronoun, (3c) must be true if (3a) is true. (3c) is true.[4] The same rule should be at work in languages with robust (strong) reflexivization, like Romance and Slavic languages, for example. Remember that passive voice is promotion of the <u>verbed</u> to preverbal position. The <u>verber</u> is demoted to a *by phrase* or deleted altogether.

This section has shown further evidence that a reflexive pronoun intransitivizes a sentence by replacing the <u>verber</u>, and the pronoun signals that the preverbal participant is the **verbed**. This rule of Spanish (and other languages) is very similar to passive voice.

2.4. If the verbed can be expressed as the subject, so can the beneficiary

Remember that the subject is said to be marked with the nominative case, the direct object with the accusative case, and the indirect object with the dative case. Thus, in (12a) in Chapter 1, The Academy is marked with the nominative, an Oscar with the accusative, and Sandra Bullock with the dative. The only remnants of case in English are in the pronoun system.[5] If *she* saw *him*, *she* is the <u>seer</u> and *him* is the **seen**; if *he* saw *her*, *he* is the <u>seer</u> and *her* is the **seen**. Thus, *she* is marked with the nominative case when *she* sees *him*, but *her* is in the accusative case when *he* sees *her*.

Interestingly, English distinguishes the subject pronouns from the object pronouns (direct, indirect, and prepositional), but the object pronouns (the last three) have all the same form: *her* could be a direct object pronoun (The Academy rewarded *her*), an indirect object pronoun (The Academy gave *her* an Oscar), or a prepositional pronoun (an Oscar went to *her*). The fact that the direct and the indirect object pronouns are the same in English accounts for the observation that there is no need to distinguish direct from indirect object in this language.[6] This observation, in turn, explains why it is so hard for native speakers of English to learn this distinction in those languages which maintain a difference between direct and indirect object, which are many of the most commonly taught second languages in the world: Arabic, Chinese, French, German, Italian, Japanese, Korean, Latin, Russian, and Spanish, to name a few.

We also saw in (12c) in Chapter 1 that the **verbed** of (12a) can be expressed as the preverbal participant in the sentence. In terms of grammatical case, the accusative has unaccusativized. If (12c) is unaccusativization, (12d) can perfectly be called undativization. In fact, a sentence like (12d) is called indirect object topicalization (expression of the indirect object as the topic in preverbal position, which is the default position for the topic).

Now we are ready to see that Italian (and other languages, including English) has a rule of undativization. Remember that we proposed above that if there is a verber (and that is true regardless of whether the sentence is transitive or intransitive), the auxiliary is *avere* 'have'. If there is not a verber, the auxiliary is *essere* 'be' (this rule is stated succinctly in 7 below). Consider now a hypothetical sentence in which Francesca has cut her finger. This is the stronger complication we promised at the end of §2.2 that we would throw at our students of Italian.

(4)   *Francesca gli ha tagliato **un dito** a Francesca.
      'Francesca has cut a finger to Francesca' (i.e. Francesca cut her finger)

Since the preverbal participant and the maleficiary are the same (Francesca), the current understanding in most theories is that the maleficiary must be replaced with a reflexive pronoun. That replacement is shown below by strike-through on the maleficiary, which is presumably replaced with the reflexive pronoun corresponding to that maleficiary. In Italian, that pronoun is *si* (the reflexive pronoun corresponding to *he, she, they, it*).

(5)   a.   *Francesca gli ha tagliato **un dito** a Francesca.
      b.   *Francesca si ha tagliato **un dito**.

The problem is that (5b) is not a sentence in Italian, although it should be, because there is apparently a verber in the sentence (Francesca), and there is also a **verbed** (un dito). The auxiliary *avere* should have been used (the sentence is transitive "on the surface"), and the past participle should be *tagliato* 'cut'. That is a serious problem for an analysis of reflexivization based on the replacement of the indirect object with the corresponding reflexive pronoun when it is identical to the subject.

If *si* is not replacing the indirect object, what is it replacing? The undativization in (12d) in Chapter 1 is the clue to solve the puzzle: the Francesca that is now in preverbal position is not the original <u>verber</u>, but the <u>maleficiary</u> promoted to subject. That analysis looks as follows:

(6) a. *<u>Francesca gli</u> ha tagliato **un dito** <u>a Francesca</u>.
b. <u>Francesca si</u> è tagliata **un dito**. (undativization, like passive voice)

This solves our problem because the preverbal participant is not the <u>verber</u>, it is the <u>maleficiary</u>. Since we already know that a sentence with a <u>verber</u> requires *avere*, we have evidence to support the claim that *si* is replacing the <u>verber</u> and that the preverbal participant in (6b) is the original <u>maleficiary</u>. That explains not only the choice of the auxiliary *essere* instead of *avere* but also agreement: the past participle agrees in number and gender with the verbed or beneficiary when there is no verber. Furthermore, the same rule of <u>verber</u> reflexivization explains the unaccusativization in (3c) in Spanish, and the undativization in (6) in Italian: the reflexive pronoun is replacing the <u>verber</u>, not the **verbed** or the <u>beneficiary</u>.[7]

Thus, a rule to explain the choice between *avere/essere* in the perfect tenses is:

(7) Use *avere* if there is a <u>verber</u> in the sentence; use *essere* otherwise.

A rule very similar to this one is used by linguists, although not with these terms. That rule cannot be used in L2 teaching due to the complexity of the terms, and the theoretical background needed to understand those terms.[8] On the other hand, with this proposal, the rule can be used in the classroom. We can now share with any learner of any L2 the fundamentally simple logic of language: the <u>verber</u> inference and the **verbed** inference. Furthermore, if we look at *Francesca ha continuato* (2b), *la lotta è continuata* (2e), and *Francesca si è tagliata un dito*, (6b), we see now that the past participle agrees with a subject that is not the <u>verber</u>. The explanation that transitive sentences take *avere* is contradicted by (5b) with an analysis based on subject, direct object, and indirect object because that sentence should take *avere*: it is transitive by virtue of having a subject in FORM (*Francesca*) and a direct object (*un dito*). With our definition of transitivity in (9) in Chapter 1, that sentence is intransitive (it has **verbed** but not <u>verber</u>), and therefore it is predicted to take *essere*.

The notion of subject does not let us see the difference in meaning of the participant in preverbal position in sentences like *Roberto worked*, *taxes increased*, and *Francesca si è tagliata un dito*. <u>Verber</u>, **verbed**, and <u>beneficiary</u> led this author to discover the difference in a language that he does not know.

The vagueness of the statement in textbooks of Italian and French (and presumably of similar languages) that many intransitive verbs take *essere* is replaced by the statement that sentences without a <u>verber</u> take the auxiliary *essere*. The generalization is that the auxiliary is *essere* if the subject is a non verber. There is no need for the stipulation that sentences with a reflexive pronoun take *essere*. <u>More importantly, the rule of agreement follows</u> from the rule of auxiliary selection in (7): <u>the past participle agrees with a non verber preverbal participant.</u>

The presence of *si* after Francesca, plus the presence of *un dito* are clear clues to the learner that Francesca is the maleficiary. If *si* replaces the <u>verber</u>, Francesca cannot be the <u>verber</u>. If those learners of Italian are native speakers of English, (8d) below will be a very close analogy (Sandra Bullock was given an Oscar). Once students understand this, they will be able to track <u>verber</u>, **verbed**, and <u>beneficiary</u> better than they can track subject, direct object, and indirect object now. Tracking three constants (<u>verber</u>, **verbed**, <u>beneficiary</u>) is easier than tracking three – or five – grammatical relations (subject, direct object, indirect object, primary object, and secondary object) that move around and hide the true function of participants on both sides of the verb (before and after).

To an extent, we are giving those students of Italian (and languages with an *avere/essere* distinction) some of the tools of a linguist to learn an L2. It takes less time to do a job with a better tool. A better tool means almost invariably a better job.

2.5. Evidence from English that the subject is the beneficiary

There is clear evidence from English that the Francesca in (6b) is the beneficiary, not the verber. The reader will remember sentences (12a-d) from Chapter 1, repeated here for convenience:

(8) a. The Academy gave an Oscar to Sandra Bullock.
     b. The Academy gave Sandra Bullock an Oscar.
     c. An Oscar was given to Sandra Bullock (by The Academy).
     d. Sandra Bullock was given an Oscar (by The Academy).

Now the reader will understand better the point made earlier that subject, direct object, and indirect object vary in syntactic variations of a sentence (as 8a-d show), yet verber, verbed, and beneficiary (maleficiary) remain constant. The Sandra Bullock in (8d) is the grammatical subject, but it is clearly still the beneficiary: she is not doing anything, and she is the recipient of an Oscar. Any speaker of English who hears or reads that *Sandra Bullock was given* knows that what is coming right after in the sentence is the given. It does not occur to any speaker of English that Sandra Bullock was given to anyone. It has not happened.

Let us consider the equivalent in Spanish of the sentences in (8):

(9) a. <u>La Academia</u> <u>le</u> dio **un Óscar** <u>a Sandra Bullock</u>. (Same as 8a)
     b. <u>La Academia</u> <u>le</u> dio <u>a Sandra Bullock</u> **un Óscar**.
     c. **Un Óscar** <u>le</u> fue dado <u>a Sandra Bullock</u> (por La Academia).
     d. <u>A Sandra Bullock</u> <u>se</u> <u>le</u> dio **un Óscar**.[9]
     e. <u>Se</u> <u>le</u> dio **un Óscar** <u>a Sandra Bullock</u>.[10]

The sentences in (9d,e) reveal several interesting points of Spanish grammar. First, they show that the reflexive pronoun is replacing the verber: (9d) is identical to (9a), except that <u>The Academy</u> is missing, and we have SE. Second, (9d,e) – called in pedagogical grammars of Spanish "unplanned occurrence" – are simply a replacement of the <u>verber</u> with the corresponding reflexive pronoun: everything is the same, and it is incorrect to claim that the "adversity" or "avoidance of responsibility" that putatively goes with those two variations of (9a) come from the construction (the combination of a reflexive pronoun followed by an indirect object pronoun). It comes from the meaning of the verb *(break, forget, die, fall, burn,* etc.), and not from *se* plus and indirect object; both of them very robust phenomena of the grammar of Spanish.[11] Third, (9d) shows the best equivalent in Spanish of the passive of an indirect object in English. In terms of this proposal, (8d) in English and (9d) are indirect object topicalizations. In terms of this proposal, that variation of (8a) can be called beneficiary topicalization.

2.6. Conclusions

The subject of a reflexive sentence that also has a **verbed** is the <u>beneficiary</u>, which has been topicalized (expressed in preverbal position as the topic of the sentence). That explains the choice of auxiliary (*essere*) and the need for that preverbal participant to agree with the past participle of the verb in Italian. Chomsky (1993: 188) formalized in his Principle A of Binding Theory an intuition from traditional grammar – going back to Greek and Latin grammars – that a reflexive pronoun is an anaphor whose antecedent is the subject (i.e. the reflexive pronoun is replacing the direct object or the indirect object to avoid an unnecessary repetition of the subject). That intuition is incorrect, and it has prevented us from seeing that the putative "subject antecedent" is really the **verbed** or the <u>beneficiary</u>.

One of the main goals of this book is to make the case that language study and language learning should be based on verber and verbed, not on subject, direct object, and indirect object. The notion of subject does not let us see the differences in the subject of sentences like *Roberto worked*, ***taxes*** *increased*, and *Francesca si è tagliata un dito*. <u>Verber</u>, **verbed**, and <u>beneficiary</u> reveal those differences. <u>Roberto</u> is the <u>worker</u> (#Roberto is the worked) and **taxes** are the **increased** (#taxes are the increaser). If the <u>Francesca</u> that we see in preverbal position is the <u>maleficiary</u>, *essere* is expected and the past participle will agree with Francesca. A rule of auxiliary selection in terms of verber, verbed, and beneficiary is simpler, more predictive, does not require open-ended lists of verbs ("many intransitive verbs take *essere*"), and above all, it does not require stipulations (reflexive sentences take *essere*). That is clear evidence that rules of language are easier to state and understand by using verber, verbed, and beneficiary. In other words, the evidence adduced so far shows that rules of languages are simpler to state and more predictive if formulated in terms of verber, verbed, and beneficiary than in terms of subject, direct object, and indirect object.

Notes

1 *Dibattito* was changed to *lotta* in order to include agreement in the discussion.
2 This rule should work for many languages. *The nominative participant in a sentence with passive voice morphology* (*be* [or *get*] + *past participle* in English) will be accurate for languages that might accept a verbed that is not before the verb (the canonical position of the verber).
3 In Spanish grammar, a reflexive pronoun replaces the direct or the indirect object when it is identical to the subject (Bello 1941[1847]: 198–199, 237; García 1975: 2, 31; RAE 1973: 208; Whitley 2002: 178, among many others). That observation goes back to Latin (perhaps Greek), where reflexive means "bending back". The intuition behind "true" reflexivity means that the reflexive pronoun refers to a previously mentioned noun (Gloria[i] saw Gloria[i] in the mirror Gloria saw herself in the mirror). The fact that this intuition was formalized by Chomsky (1993: 188) as Principle A of Binding Theory is evidence that this is the analysis in most languages and in most linguistic theories.
4 Whitley & González (2016) is the first textbook for Spanish as an L2 that explains reflexivization as verber deletion.
5 Cases are "visible" in endings in nouns in some languages. German, Finnish, Polish, etc., still have traces of those endings. Prepositions have replaced some or all of those endings in many languages.
6 There are no traces of grammatical case in nouns in English. The difference between *who* and *whom* is a remnant of the distinction between subject and object. In terms of this proposal, *who* is the pronoun for a verber; *whom*, for a

non verber. The other remnant of case is the distinction between subject pronouns (*she*) and non subject pronouns (*her*).

7 Spanish also has a rule of undativization with a reflexive pronoun:

    i. Francesca se ha cortado un dedo.
       'Francesca has cut her finger(herself)'
    ii. A Francesca se le cortó un dedo.
       'Someone cut one of Francesca's fingers'

    Interestingly, (i) would favor a reading in which she ended up with a cut in one of her fingers; (ii) would favor a reading in which one of her fingers got severed.

8 Using subject, direct object, and indirect object, only linguists (or advanced graduate students of linguistics) understand the Unaccusativity Hypothesis, and an analysis of auxiliary selection based on it.

9 Since *se* is replacing the verber, the prediction is that *by The Academy* should make the sentence ungrammatical in Spanish. That prediction is correct.

10 Intuitively, (9d) should be more frequent than (9e).

11 The *se me* construction is a complex issue in the grammar of Spanish. See Bull (1965: 265–274); García (1975); Schmitz (1966); Whitley (2002: 183–184) and Whitley & González (2016), among many others, for some discussion.

References

Bello, Andrés. 1941[1847]. *Gramática de la lengua castellana*. With notes by Rufino J. Cuervo. Buenos Aires: Librería Perlado Editores.

Bull, William E. 1965. *Spanish for teachers. Applied linguistics*. New York: The Ronald Press Company.

Chomsky, Noam. 1993. *Lectures on government and binding. The Pisa lectures*. Berlin: Mouton de Gruyter.

García, Erica C. 1975. *The role of theory in linguistic analysis: The Spanish pronoun system*. Amsterdam: North-Holland.

RAE (Real Academia Española). 1973. *Esbozo de una gramática de la lengua española*. 21st reprint. Madrid: Espasa.

Rosen, Carol. 1984. The interface between semantic roles and initial grammatical relations. In Perlmutter, David M. & Rosen, Carol (eds.), *Studies in relational grammar*, vol. 2, 38–77. Chicago: The University of Chicago Press.

Schmitz, John Robert. 1966. The *se me* construction: Reflexive for unplanned occurrences. *Hispania* 49(3). 430–433. (https://www.jstor.org/stable/337456).

Whitley, M. Stanley. 2002. *Spanish/English contrasts. A course in Spanish linguistics*. 2nd ed. Washington, DC: Georgetown University Press. (http://press .georgetown.edu/book/languages/spanishenglish-contrasts).

Whitley, M. Stanley & González, Luis. 2016. *Gramática para la composición*. 3a ed. Washington, DC: Georgetown University Press.

3 Solving the transitivity paradox

3.1. Introduction

Chapter 1 showed that a sentence is transitive if it has a verber and a verbed, and that it is intransitive if it has either a verber or a verbed, but not both. It also showed that the verber is always the subject, but the subject is not always the verber because if there is no verber, the verbed is "promoted" to subject. When a sentence has verber and verbed, the verber tends to be a person and the verbed tends to be a thing. It is more accurate to state that the verber tends to be animate and the verbed tends to be inanimate.[1] Animate covers not only humans but also deities, animals, and "personified" objects or concepts. However, for simplicity and intuitiveness, and because more often than not *animate* refers to human, we will use the notation [+H] and [-H], an abbreviation for [+Human] and [-Human]. [+H] means that the REFERENT is human or animate and [-H] means that the referent is inanimate.[2]

> REFERENT: The being, object, or concept a word refers to. The object that the reader is reading (on paper or in electronic form) is the referent for the object called *book* in English. A witty definition for REFERENT is *what in the world a word refers to.*

Now we can state that the verber tends to be [+H] and the verbed tends to be [-H]. Thus, if one wants to represent this as an alignment of a [+H] verber and a [-H] verbed, (1a) below will be the typical alignment.[3]

The possible combinations of animacy ([+H], [-H]) and verber and verbed give the three atypical alignments of animacy in (1b-d).[4] If we wanted a name for this alignment, a good one would be the VERBER/**VERBED** ANIMACY ALIGNMENT. For the sake of simplicity, we will simply call it the ANIMACY ALIGNMENT. To my knowledge, nobody has noticed the three marked alignments in (1b-d) below, and nobody has put them together as in (1a-d) below. This animacy alignment will play an important role in our explanation of the transitivity paradox, "personal *a*", and *leísmo* in Spanish.[5]

verber **verbed**

(1) a. [+H], [-H] Typical alignment of verber, **verbed**
    b. [-H], [+H] Atypical alignment
    c. [+H], [+H] Atypical alignment
    d. [-H], [-H] Atypical alignment

Let us consider a famous pair of verbs in English (*fear* and *frighten*) and apply to them the verber and **verbed** inferences. I have added the passive voice in (2b) and (3b) as evidence that these verbs are transitive in English. Passive voice is a highly reliable indicator of transitivity.

(2) a. Students fear tests.
    b. **Tests** are feared by students. Passive. (cf. #Students are feared by tests)
    c. Students are the fearer. (cf. #Students are the feared)
    d. **Tests** are the **feared**. (cf. #Tests are the fearer)

(3) a. Tests frighten **students**. → transitiva .
    b. **Students** are frightened by tests. Passive. (cf. #Tests are frightened by students)
    c. Tests are the frightener. (cf. #Students are the frightener)
    d. **Students** are the **frightened**. (cf. #Tests are the frightened)

These two verbs belong to two different classes of PSYCHOLOGICAL verbs (defined below). At least one of the participants must be [+H], but both can be ANIMATE. However, most discussions of these verbs focus on sentences with a [+H] participant and a [-H] participant. In fact, *fear* verbs are referred to as Stimulus-object verbs (the object – *tests* – is the stimulus [for (2a) only, of course]) and *frighten* verbs are Stimulus-subject verbs (now *tests* is the subject).[6] That distinction was needed before the present proposal. If you are not a linguist, chances are that you have no idea that this distinction has been proposed. Interestingly, native speakers (and advanced second language learners of English) can use these two verbs without being aware of the distinction. When I tell my students that they cannot frighten tests, although it would be nice to scare the heck out of them, they get the joke. That adds to the evidence that the verber and **verbed** inferences are the heart of the fundamentally simple logic of language.

PSYCHOLOGICAL (PSYCH) VERBS: verbs that express cognition, emotion, or perception. Psych verbs have been a headache for theories of LINKING or ARGUMENT REALIZATION. For the last 50 years, most linguistic theories invoke informally (and some formally) a role of EXPERIENCER, the [+H] who experiences an emotion (as subject, as with *fear*, or as direct object, as with *frighten*).[7] A role of EXPERIENCER is not needed with the <u>verber</u> and **verbed** inferences, as Chapters 3–6 show.

LINKING THEORY (ARGUMENT STRUCTURE or ARGUMENT REALIZATION): the branch of linguistics that deals with the problem of who is the subject, the direct object, and the indirect object. When semantic roles were introduced in linguistics, linguists began referring to semantic roles as the issue of "who does what to whom in a sentence". This author has been unable to trace this quote. When I asked M. Stanley Whitley, a scholar who has used it for over 20 years, he said that he might have been the one who came up with that clever wording (p.c. 2018).

This is a good point to introduce briefly the term <u>VERBEE</u>. We have referred to the referent of the indirect object as the *<u>beneficiary</u>* or *<u>maleficiary</u>*, terms that most speakers understand in context, even if they have not read or heard them. To my knowledge, Gil (1982) was the first scholar to refer to the indirect object of verbs like *belong, happen, matter, occur*, etc., as the <u>BENEFACTEE</u> or <u>MALEFACTEE</u>. A fitting generalization would be the <u>VERBEE</u>, a term that Chapter 4 will explain in more detail. Readers will be able to follow the discussion knowing that <u>verbee</u> is a generalization over <u>beneficiary</u> (<u>benefactee</u>) and <u>maleficiary</u> (<u>malefactee</u>). <u>Verbee</u> also covers the indirect object of any sentence with <u>verber</u>, **verbed**, and <u>verbee</u>. Sandra Bullock was the <u>awardee</u> (<u>verbee</u>) when <u>she</u> was given **an Oscar**.

Returning to *fear* and *frighten*, these verbs are famous in linguistics because in languages that have kept a distinction between **verbeds** and <u>verbees</u> (direct object and indirect object), the equivalent of at least one of these verbs tends to mark its only object (the **verbed**) as if it were a <u>verbee</u>. In terms of accusative (direct object) and dative (indirect object), it is as if the verb had an indirect object, not a direct object. In terms of accusative and dative, if there is not a participant marked with the accusative (a direct object) in a sentence, that sentence is intransitive.[8]

3.2. The problem: sentences that are intransitive by case but transitive by meaning

Observe the following case marking or transitivity paradox in the equivalent in Spanish of sentence (3) above: The same sentence can have a subject and an indirect object or a subject and a direct object, *without* a difference in meaning.[9] In our terms, the object can be a <u>verbee</u> or a **verbed**:

(4) a. <u>A las estudiantes les</u>   asustan <u>los exámenes.</u>
        (DAT, NOM)[10]   (intransitive)
        To the students   DAT frighten the tests
        'Tests frighten students'. (Lit: 'to the students, tests frighten')
     b. **A las estudiantes las**   asustan <u>los exámenes.</u>
        (ACC, NOM)   (transitive)
        To the students   ACC frighten the tests
     c. <u>Los exámenes</u> asustan **a las estudiantes.**
        (NOM, ACC)   (transitive)
     d. <u>Los exámenes les</u> asustan **a las estudiantes.**
        (NOM, DAT)   (intransitive)

When the sentence has a subject and a direct object, as in (4b,c), the sentence is transitive. When the sentence has an indirect object and a subject as in (4a) or a subject and an indirect object, as in (4d), the sentence is intransitive. (With most verbs, the order *indirect object, subject* is more frequent than *subject, indirect object*, and there is no difference in meaning. §5.4 will address this issue). This is a case marking paradox (direct object/indirect object paradox) that goes back to Latin. The <u>verber</u> and **verbed** inferences solve this paradox.

3.3. The solution to the paradox

Let us apply the <u>verber</u> inference as in (6a) and the **verbed** inference as in (6b) to (4a,c), repeated here as (5a,b). (5a) [=4a] is uncontroversially marked as an indirect object (DAT); (5b) [=4c] is uncontroversially marked as a direct object (ACC).

(5) a. <u>A las estudiantes</u> LES asustan <u>los exámenes.</u>
        to the students-DAT DAT-CLITIC frighten the exams-NOM
        'To students, tests are frightening'. (Tests frighten students)
     b. <u>Los exámenes</u> asustan **a las estudiantes.**
        NOM   ACC
        'Tests frighten students'.
(6) a. <u>Los exámenes</u> son <u>los asustadores.</u>   (Verber inference)
        'Tests are the frighteners'.
     b. **Las estudiantes** son **las asustadas.**   (Verbed inference)
        'Students are the frightened'.

    c. (cf. #<u>Los exámenes</u> son **los asustados.**)[11]
       #'Tests are the frightened'.
    d. (cf. #**Las estudiantes** son <u>las asustadoras.</u>)
       #'Students are the frighteners'.

The <u>verber</u> and **verbed** inferences show that the sentence is transitive. Remember that the equivalent in English of (5a,b) are clearly transitive. In addition to the <u>verber</u> and **verbed** inferences, there are four other entailments that most transitive sentences satisfy, and those four entailments confirm that (7a) [=5a] is transitive, even when it has an "indirect object" (instead of a direct object), as (7b-e) show.

(7) a. <u>A las estudiantes</u> <u>LES</u> asustan <u>los exámenes</u>.
       'Tests frighten students'.
    b. **Las estudiantes** <u>se</u> asustan con/por (=a causa de) los exámenes. (Unaccusativization)
       'Students were (got) frightened by the tests'.
    c. **A las estudiantes las** asustan <u>los exámenes</u>. (Direct object topicalization)
       'To students, tests are frightening'.
    d. **Las estudiantes** son asustadas por los exámenes. (Passive = unaccusativization)
       'Students are frightened by tests'.
    e. **Las estudiantes** están asustadas.[12] (Resultative sentence)
       'The students are frightened'. (Students are in a state of fright)

On the other hand, an intransitive sentence; that is, one whose only object must be an indirect object, does not allow any of the previous four entailments in (7b-e), as (8b-e) show:[13]

(8) a. <u>A las estudiantes</u> <u>les</u> gustan **los exámenes**
       DAT   NOM
       'Students like tests'.
    b. *<u>Las estudiantes</u> se gustan con/por (=a causa de) los exámenes.
       *'Students are liked by tests'.
    c. *<u>A las estudiantes</u> **las** gustan **los exámenes**.
       #'Tests like students'.
    d. *<u>Las estudiantes</u> son gustadas por los exámenes.
       #'Students are liked by tests'.
    e. *<u>Las estudiantes</u> están gustadas.
       *'Students are in a state of liking'. ("Likingness")

Readers unfamiliar with languages in which *gustar* is intransitive will see the difference if we use *matter*, as (9) shows:

(9) a. **Tests**   matter <u>to students</u>.
Test-NOM matter to-students-DAT
   b. *<u>Students</u> themselves matter with/because of tests.
   c. *<u>Tests</u> matter **students**.
   d. *<u>Students</u> are mattered by tests.
   e. *<u>Students</u> are mattered. (Students are in a state of "matterness")

With that evidence for the transitivity of (5a,b), regardless of the marking of the direct object (**las estudiantes**) with dative, a question arises. If (5a) is transitive by *six* entailments (6a,b and 7b-e), how do we account for its NOM, DAT marking in (5a)? That is, how do we account for the fact that **a las estudiantes** in (5a) appears to be an indirect object?

With a rule of <u>DATIVE OVERRIDING</u> OF THE ACCUSATIVE proposed in González (1997). Dative overriding means that a **direct object** (the accusative) looks to the native speaker as if it were an <u>indirect object</u> (the dative), and therefore the speaker uses (marks) **the direct object** as if it were <u>an indirect object</u>. The indirect object overrides the "mark" of the direct object; <u>the indirect object</u> imposes its mark on **the direct object**. This rule explains true or general *LEÍSMO* as a rule in the grammar of every speaker of Spanish, not only as a dialectal phenomenon commonly associated only with speakers of central and northern Spain.[14] There is evidence for this rule in Latin, German, Japanese, and English, and presumably in many other languages. Such a rule can be stated as follows:

(10) <u>Dative</u> Overriding of the **Accusative**:

An **accusative** (a direct object) <u>tends to be marked with dative</u> (as an indirect object) when it is as high in animacy as the <u>nominative</u> (12c,d), and particularly when it is higher (12b).

In terms of verber, verbed, verbee, that rule can be stated as follows:

(11) <u>Dative</u> Overriding of the **Accusative**:

A **verbed** tends to be marked as if it were a <u>verbee</u> when it is as high in animacy as the <u>verber</u> (12c,d), and particularly when it is higher (12b).

We repeat here for convenience the animacy alignments in (1a-d) as (12a-d):

<u>verber</u> **verbed**

(12) a.   [+H] , [-H] Typical Animacy Alignment of <u>verber</u>, **verbed**
   b.   [-H] , [+H] Atypical alignment
   c.   [+H] , [+H] Atypical alignment
   d.   [-H] , [-H] Atypical alignment

3.4. Dative overriding in four languages belonging to three different families

What is the evidence for dative overriding of the accusative? In many languages in the world, a [+H] direct object tends to be marked as an "indirect object" when the subject is [-H]; that is, in the alignment in (12b). The following example from Latin has a [-H] subject and a [+H] direct object. We know that this sentence is transitive because it entails that <u>fortune</u> is the <u>favorer</u> and **the brave** is the **favored** in English, in Spanish, and presumably in Latin. The alignment in (12b) is atypical because the direct object is [+H]. Since indirect objects are overwhelmingly [+H] in most languages in the world, there is motivation for the rule of dative overriding to apply. The intuition at work seems to be that a [+H] direct object looks like an "indirect object". At least two factors are at play: animacy and definiteness.[15] Hopper & Thompson (1980: 259) report that in a text in English in which they identified 33 indirect objects, 100% of them were not only animate but also human and definite.

(13) Fortuna   favet   fortibus
   fortune-NOM favor-3sg brave-DAT
   'Fortune favors the brave' (Latin proverb, Van Hoecke 1996: 7).

The following example from German, a language from a different family, also has dative overriding. The object is [+H] and the subject is [-H]:

(14) Mir   ekelt   vor   fetten Speisen.   (German)
   1sg-pro-DAT nauseate before fat   food
   'Fat food nauseates me'. (Draye 1996: 193)

The only object in sentences with the equivalent in German of each of the following verbs (among many others) is marked with the dative: *answer, believe, congratulate, encounter, damage, follow, impress, hurt, succeed, threaten*, etc. Those verbs behave exactly the same in Spanish. What do they have in common? The object is [+H]. If that human is a true indirect object (*answer, believe*), it must be marked as a verbee. If it is a human direct object, it will often be marked as a verbee (*congratulate, encounter, follow, impress, succeed, threaten*, etc.). Some of those verbs have a true verbee (in addition to a **verbed**, which is often omitted with a few verbs), as §5.5 shows. If you answer **a question** to someone (or someone's question), you simply answer someone (**a question**); if you believe **what** someone told (to) you, you believe someone (**what they told you**); if you damaged my reputation, you "damaged the reputation to me", you caused me to lose my reputation; if you hurt my feelings (hurt the feelings "to me"), my feelings were hurt, you hurt me. Those are true verbees; the **verbed** was left out. On the other hand, some of those verbs have just one object, a [+H] **verbed**: you encounter **someone**, you threaten **him** or **her**, you follow or succeed **the director**, you impress **that person** at a party, etc. That human object is marked as if it were a verbee, but it is really a [+H] **verbed.**

According to traditional Spanish grammar (RAE 2010: 316), some verbs that can use *le* or *lo* to refer to a direct object, admitted dative already in Latin ("ya admitían dativo en latín"). All of those verbs have a [+H] only object. The fact that they were expressed using an indirect object (the dative case) instead of a direct object (the accusative case) does not have to be stipulated. Dative overriding not only predicts it; it explains it because it is an atypical animacy alignment. It is accurate to state that the verbs from German in the preceding paragraph are "dative admitters". We can take these facts as a coincidence in three languages belonging to two different families. Or we can look at this phenomenon as a rule of dative overriding at work in several languages. There is strong evidence for the second option. In fact, dative overriding might be a rule of hundreds of languages. As explained in Chapter 2, speakers of English know that one can refer to a rejected boyfriend or girlfriend as a **dumpee**, but it is hard to imagine a dumpster truck loaded with dumpees. Unless someone wants to prove me wrong on this one and goes to the trouble of loading a truck with dumpees. I would not be surprised to see a cartoon about this on the Internet. It was not there when I wrote this. The contents of a dumpster truck unloaded at a dumpster site will be called a dumped load, never a dumpee.

The alignment of a [-H] subject and a [+H] direct object is also what we see in (4a) [=7a] in Spanish. Thus, we have evidence from three different languages for a rule of dative overriding. In the three languages, the subject is [-H] and the "dative" object is [+H], the atypical alignment in (12b).

There is a dialectal phenomenon in Spanish called *LEÍSMO*. In a few words, it is the use of the indirect object pronoun *le* instead of the direct object pronoun *lo* to refer to a direct object, as the cell in bold shows in the following table.

Although the literature on *leísmo* is extensive, the common understanding is that *le* can be used instead of *lo* when the direct object is singular, and

Table 3.1 Subject, direct, and indirect object pronouns in Spanish

	Subject pronoun	Direct object	Indirect object
I	Yo	Me	Me
You (informal)	Tú	Te	Te
You (formal)	Usted	Lo/la	Le
He	Él	Lo (**le**)	Le
She	Ella	La	Le
We	Nosotros/nosotras	Nos	Nos
You (informal)	Vosotros/vosotras	Os	Os
You (formal)	Ustedes	Los	Les
They	Ellos/ellas	Los/las	Les

masculine. According to RAE (1973: 204–205), the use of *le* instead of *lo* is presumably due to:

> [...] una tendencia de la lengua a introducir en el pronombre de 3.a persona una diferenciación genérica: *le* para el acusativo masculino, *la* para el femenino, *lo* para el neutro, a costa de la diferenciación casual. Pero la tendencia no llega a su pleno desarrollo. El dativo neutro *le* se mantiene inalterable. No prospera tanto el acusativo plural *les* como el singular *le*.[16]

The most convincing explanation for *leísmo*, in my opinion, is that the series *lo/lo/le* (direct object/neuter/indirect object) for a *masculine* referent does not contrast as well as the series *la/lo/le* (direct object/neuter/indirect object), the series for a *feminine* referent. The plural *les* instead of *los* is less frequent because the series would be *los/lo/les* and *las/lo/les*, and each of those two series is clearly contrastive (Fernández Ramírez 1987: 43–44). That reasoning is questionable, however, because when *leísmo* is applied to a masculine, singular referent, we end up with the series *le/lo/le* (direct object/neuter/indirect object), which is equally as uncontrastive as *lo/lo/le*. The question as to why *le* instead of *la* is a lot less common than *le* instead of *lo* (dialectal *leísmo*) is an issue begging for a fresh set of eyes.

In the following sentence, most native speakers in 21 out of 22 countries will use *la* for Isabel and *lo* for Fernando, but speakers from León and Castilla in Spain will use *le* for Fernando.

(15) a.   ¿Viste a Isabel y a Fernando?
      'Did you see Isabel and Fernando?'

  b.   *Le/La   vi   a ella, pero no le/lo   vi   a él.
      DAT-pro/ACC-pro see-1sg-past to her but no DAT-pro/ACC-pro see-1sg-past to him
      'I saw her, but I did not see him'.

Dialectal *Leísmo* "accounts for" the alignment in (12c), but only when the direct object is singular and masculine. That is actually not a rule but a "gender difference" that missed woman, women, and men out of woman, women, men, and man. One cannot help but think that it is the result of a confusion, which dates back to Medieval and classical texts. Lapesa (1983: 405) observed that *leísmo* was already present in *El mío Cid* (circa 1200). *Leísmo* (but just for a masculine singular referent) appeared so frequently that The Royal Academy of the Spanish Language *declared* in 1796 that it was the only correct use for the accusative masculine (Lapesa 1983: 471). The Academy later recognized that the distinction between *le/lo* was a more general rule, that it was to be preferred, and changed its "declaration" to a "toleration" that is still accepted today. The reason why I used a feminine plural referent in example (4a) is because a feminine plural *las* is the complete opposite of a masculine singular *lo*, and it cannot be explained with dialectal *leísmo*, but can be explained with dative overriding. (4a) is repeated below as (16):

(16) **A las estudiantes**   les   asustan los exámenes.
      to the-fem students DAT frighten the tests
      'Tests frighten students'.

Dative overriding is the big picture: a [+H] **verbed** highly favors being marked as a verbee when the subject is an inanimate referent. And marking that direct object (*la/las/lo/los*) as if it were an indirect object (*le/les*) is the rule – no pun intended – in 22 out of 22 Spanish speaking countries, not only for a feminine, plural referent as exemplified in (16), but for any animate referent, regardless of gender or number. This is dative overriding of the accusative due to the atypical animacy alignment in (12b), without unwanted restrictions. *Aburrir* 'bore', *fascinar* 'fascinate', *molestar* 'bother', *preocupar* 'worry', among many other verbs, are verbs commonly thought (and taught) to belong in Spanish to the *gustar* class (RAE 2010: 680) because their only object is "indirect" instead of direct. Dative overriding predicts that if **a mis amigas** passes the **verbed** inference (as in 17 below), **a mis amigas** can also be marked as if it were a direct object. That prediction is correct: speakers use les in (17a) more frequently than **las**, but the latter is also possible. (17b) can have les, and that means that the speaker is marking **a mis amigas** as if it were an indirect object. However, the les can be omitted, and that means that the speaker is marking (perceiving, or "conceptualizing", as Ray Jackendoff would write) **a mis amigas** as if it were a direct object. The order in (17a) is more common than that in (17b) because it privileges animacy (it expresses the animate participant in preverbal position, the canonical position of the animate participant).

(17) a. **A mis amigas**   les/**las**   aburre/fascina/molesta/preocupa
leer mis borradores.
to my friends-fem DAT/ACC bore/fascinate/bother/worry
reading my drafts.
'Reading my drafts bores/fascinates/bothers/worries my friends'.
'Reading my drafts is boring/fascinating/bothering/worrying to
my friends'.

b. Leer mis borradores (les) aburre/fascina/molesta/preocupa **a mis
amigas**.

The following examples come from Japanese, a language from a third different family. Sentence (18a) takes a direct object, as the marker *o* indicates;
(18b,c) take an indirect object, as the marker *ni* indicates.[17]

(18) a. watashi-wa anata-o odorokasu.
I-NOM   you-ACC surprised
'I surprised you'. — d. o.
b. watashi-wa anata-ni au.
I-NOM   you-DAT met
'I met you'.
c. watashi-wa anata-ni akogareru.
I-NOM   you-DAT admire
'I admire you'. — i. o.

Thus, native speakers of English that feel annoyed, bothered, confused, daz-
zled, frustrated, or irritated when they have to distinguish direct from indirect
objects in other languages can find some consolation in the fact that if we
use these terms (or accusative and dative), and if we do not know that the
dative overrides the accusative, it is extremely difficult to see the distinction,
even for scholars, as this section has shown for Latin, German, Spanish, and
Japanese. The difficulty was real. Being able to see that distinction for the
first time thanks to the verber and verbed inferences is part of the fundamentally simple logic of language.

There is evidence of dative overriding in Spanish for the alignment in (12d);
that is, when both subject and direct object are [-H]. If the pronoun *le(s)* is
used in the following sentences, the speaker is applying dative overriding;
if the speaker uses ***la(s)*** or ***lo(s)***, the speaker is not applying dative overriding. The meaning of each sentence is the same, regardless of the use of the
indirect object or the direct object pronoun.

(19) a. Al   amor le/lo   acompaña   la
locura. (Al = a + el [to + the])
to-DAT/ACC-the love, DAT/ACC-pronoun accompanies the
madness
'Madness accompanies love'.
b. A La Paz le/la sigue Santa Cruz en población.[18]
'Santa Cruz follows La Paz in population'.
c. A la letra *a* le/la sigue la letra *b*.
'Letter *b* follows letter *a*'.
d. En CofC, a la *o* le/la precede una *c* y le/la sigue una *f*, la cual precede a la otra *c*.
'In CofC, a *c* precedes the *o* and (the *o*) is followed by an *f*, which
precedes the other *c*'.
e. Al 2025 le/lo seguirá el 2026.
'(The year) 2026 will follow (the year) 2025'.

Why should there be a "verbee"/**verbed** alternation with a [-H] subject and
a [-H] object? Because it is an atypical animacy alignment. Observe the
following possible alternations of (19a) in Spanish. Those familiar with
Spanish will be able to see why the sentences with TOPICALIZATION
will be easier to process: they all make it easier to understand an atypical alignment. Why *le(s)* instead of *la(s)/lo(s)*? Because many of those
topicalized non verbers are higher than or as high in the animacy alignment as the verber. In either case, dative (*le/les*) is favored over accusative
(*la/las; lo/los*) since Latin; and not only in Spanish, but presumably in
other languages.

TOPICALIZATION is the expression of the object (direct or indirect) before
the verb. Since the verber is the TOPIC of the sentence, and it precedes the
verb in the typical word order, when either the **direct object** or the indirect
object is expressed before the verb, it is said to be topicalized. Thus, there
is **direct object** topicalization or indirect object topicalization. In terms of
this proposal, there is **verbed** topicalization (***An Oscar*** *was given to Sandra
Bullock*), and verbee topicalization (*Sandra Bullock was given an Oscar*).

---

(20) a. %La locura acompaña **el amor**.   (2 hits. Google. 3/12/16)
b. La locura acompaña **al amor**.   (492 hits. Google. 3/12/16)
c. **Al amor lo** acompaña la locura.   (7 hits. Google. 3/12/16)
d. **Al amor le** acompaña la locura.   (1 hit. Google. 3/12/16)
e. *La locura **lo** acompaña **al amor**.   (0 hits. Google. 3/12/16)
f. La locura le acompaña **al amor**.

In Spanish, there is as much reason to require *a* before a [+H] **verbed** (a direct object), due to the fact that the **verbed** could be the <u>verber</u>, as there is when both <u>verber</u> and **verbed** are [-H]. When that *a* is necessary, that **verbed** tends to be expressed before the verb, and clitic doubling (*la/lo/las/los/le/les*) is mandatory. Now we have two grammar clues (flags) indicating to the listener or reader that the preverbal participant is not the <u>verber</u>, and that the non verber is special (atypical) vis-à-vis the verber.[19] We will explore the motivation for that in more detail in §3.7 below. The reader will see with sentence (25) why (20a) is so infrequent vis-à-vis (20b).

Thus far, we have seen evidence of dative overriding in four different languages (Latin, German, Japanese, Spanish) belonging to three different families. We have also seen that dative overriding applies to the atypical alignments of (12b-d).

3.5. Dative overriding in English (*leísmo* in English)

As Chapter 2 showed, there is evidence of dative overriding in nouns derived from a verb in English. A noun derived from a [+H] direct object takes *–ee*, the suffix used to form nouns out of indirect objects in English (<u>addressee</u>, <u>grantee</u>, <u>payee</u>, <u>licensee</u>, etc.) as the nouns in (21) show:

(21) Appointee, callee, detainee, dumpee, escapee, invitee, kissee, nominee, etc.

What is the difference between the nouns in (21) and nouns like <u>grantee</u>, <u>licensee</u>, <u>payee</u>? The same as that between **an Oscar** and <u>Sandra Bullock</u>: the **appointee** = the **appointed official**; the **callee** = the **called person**; the **detainee** = the **detained accused**; the **dumpee** = the **dumped boyfriend/girlfriend**, etc. On the other hand, the <u>addressee</u> ≠ the **written message**; the <u>grantee</u> ≠ the **granted money**; the <u>payee</u> ≠ the **paid money**, the <u>licensee</u> ≠ the **licensed product**. This nominalization takes place not only with the object of a transitive sentence. It also takes place with a [+H] object of prepositional sentences (a sentence whose only object is a phrase introduced by a preposition, as when <u>one</u> depends **on someone**):

(22) Barkee, experimentee, gazee, laughee, etc.

These are, of course, the person barked at, experimented on, gazed at, laughed at, etc. It is very infrequent to find nominalizations of human objects with other than the *–ee* suffix in English. Jespersen (1905: 111) observed over a century ago that "*vendee* is the man to whom something is sold", when he was explaining that the *–ee* suffix came to English from French, a language that has kept alive in form its direct and indirect object distinction much more than English. Notice the efficiency in language in adopting the *–ee* suffix: one word (*vendee*) instead of seven (the person to whom something is sold). A handful of nouns in English show this efficiency in language particularly well. What is a <u>committee</u>? A group of people to whom an issue is sent for consideration (12 words). A <u>referee</u> is a person or group to whom a dispute is sent for arbitration (12 words). An <u>amputee</u> is a person (or animal) who has had a limb (or more) amputated.

3.6. Case created the transitivity paradox; verber and verbed solve it

The explanation provided for the <u>verbee</u>/**verbed** alternation answers the question at the beginning of this chapter: sentences with an only object marked as if it were an indirect object are transitive if that object passes the **verbed** inference. That **verbed** tends to be marked as a <u>verbee</u> when it is as high and particularly when it is higher in animacy than the <u>verber</u>. Of course, that **verbed** can be expressed as a direct object in the sentence. We have solved the case marking paradox by using the <u>verber</u> and **verbed** inferences, two inferences that capture the essence of the UNACCUSATIVE HYPOTHESIS, the discovery that the subject of some intransitive sentences is not the <u>verber</u>.[20] Thus, there are two main types of intransitive sentences. For type one, the subject is a <u>verber</u> (<u>Roberto</u> worked); for type two, the subject is a **verbed** (taxes **increased**). *The notion of subject has blurred for 21 centuries a distinction that the verber and* **verbed** *inferences bring out.* An explicit awareness (repetition intended) of the verber and verbed inferences is part of the fundamentally simple logic of language that makes L1 learning much more effortless and efficient than L2 learning. Now L2 learners can use that tool to their advantage.

We have used entailments, simple inferences that all speakers use (without knowing it), to solve the transitivity paradox and to explain the Unaccusative Hypothesis in a way that college and high school students will understand. The only new concept is a rule of dative overriding, a rule for which we have shown ample evidence and a great deal of motivation:

(23) a. It applies to the atypical alignments of subject and direct object in (1b-d).

   b. It makes it possible to propose a definition of transitivity whose simplicity explains why children use subject, direct object, and indirect object without any instruction before they go to Kindergarten.[21]

   c. It shows that dialectal *leísmo* is part of a bigger phenomenon, *general leísmo*. See §3.7 below.

   d. It explains "personal *a*" in Spanish with the same rule of *leísmo*, as §3.7 below shows.[22]

   e. It makes direct and indirect object completely predictable, at least in Spanish and English.[23]

For those with some background in linguistics:

    Unergativity/unaccusativity is perhaps the most famous split in linguistics. Relatively few people understand it, and it requires a comparison of different languages – actually, different language families – and rather complex information, some of it implicit. For example, the fact that a direct object in English cannot be distinguished from a subject, unless both are pronouns (me ≠ I), but even some pronouns share the same form for subject, direct object, indirect object, *and* prepositional object: <u>You</u> [subject] *know* **me** but *I might not know* **you** [direct object]. With <u>verber</u>/**verbed**, the main point of unergativity/unaccusativity can now be understood by high school students studying an L2. One of the main proposals of this book is that an understanding of verber/verbed is tantamount to giving college and high school students of an L2 an understanding of case and semantic roles that only linguists have. This sounds like a grandiose statement. It is very ambitious, but this proposal is built on empirical evidence, not on any theoretical constructs. There are no assumptions in this proposal. Not even primitives. The verber and verbed inferences are two simple inferences that do not have to be taught, clear evidence that they are part of universal grammar. Verber/verbed/verbee are read from the morphology of a few languages looked at in some detail so far.

    As Chapters 4 and 5 will show, there is no need to invoke "inherent" or "lexical" dative. With verber, verbed, verbee, case is completely predictable, at least in English and Spanish. Presumably in many other languages. Since dative is marked with a preposition, it need not be part of a theory of linking or argument structure. §4.5 explains why.

3.7. Connecting *leísmo* and "accusative *a*"

What does dative overriding have to do with an *a* required in Spanish before a direct object when [+H]?[24] Readers familiar with Spanish might have been wondering whether this analysis was missing "personal *a*" (part of differential object marking). Consider again sentence (19a), repeated as (24a), but this time we will show several possible syntactic variations of it (24b-f), including one ungrammatical (23d), one unlikely (24e), and one infrequent (24f):

(24) a. **Al amor** le acompaña <u>la locura</u>. (1 hit. Google. 3/12/16)
    b. **Al amor** lo acompaña <u>la locura</u>. (7 hits. Google. 3/12/16)
    c. <u>La locura</u> acompaña **al amor**. (492 hits. Google. 3/12/16)
    d. *<u>La locura</u> **lo** acompaña **al amor**. (0 hits. Google. 3/12/16)
    e. %<u>La locura</u> acompaña **el amor**. (2 hits. Google. 3/12/16)
    f. <u>La locura</u> le acompaña **al amor**.[25]

Sentences (24a-c) are grammatical. They all have "personal *a*". The frequency of each is indicated in parenthesis.[26] The first one has not only "personal *a*" but also dative overriding. Personal *a* is not necessarily "personal", but it is required or at least favored when the direct object is equal in animacy to the subject, and particularly when the former is higher.[27] Those are the atypical alignments in (1c,d). Observe that duplication with an indirect object pronoun (or with a direct object pronoun) is mandatory when the *non verber* is preverbal, as in (24a,b), but it is ungrammatical with a direct object pronoun when postverbal, as in (24d). However, it is not ungrammatical with an indirect object pronoun, as in (24f), which intuitively seems rather infrequent. Except for (25c), the following examples are attested with an indirect object pronoun, with a direct object pronoun, and, of course, with "personal *a*". The reader is invited to reconstruct the equivalent of the variants in (24b-d) above for each of the sentences in (25).

(25) a. **A** La Paz **le/la** sigue Santa Cruz en población.[28]
    b. A la *a* **le/la** sigue la *b*.
    c. En CofC, a la *o* **le/la** precede una *c* y **le/la** sigue una *f*, la cual precede a la otra *c*.
    d. Al 2025 **le/lo** seguirá el 2026.

Since the order of a *direct object* preceding the *subject* is conceivably almost as frequent in Spanish as the *subject* preceding the *direct object* when both participants are equal in animacy, sentence (24e) would be ambiguous, or at least more difficult to process than a sentence with a [+H] verber and a [-H] verbed. If it were not because sentences with [–H] subject and [-H] object are relatively infrequent, sentence (24e) might be as unacceptable as (26), which virtually no native speaker of Spanish says or writes:

(26) *Pedro vio Penélope cuando ella tenía 19 años.
    'Peter saw Penélope when she was 19 years old'.

According to pedagogical grammars of Spanish, the intuition is that Penélope requires "personal *a*" because she might have been the one who saw Pedro. With the animacy alignment, there is a good explanation as to why Spanish speakers virtually never fail to use "personal *a*" in sentences like (26), even when one of the participants is singular and the other plural, a case in which ambiguity should not arise.[29] In fact, the same is true for (24e). Furthermore, direct object topicalization appears to be the preferred way of expressing sentences whose object is [+H]. If true, the rule would be that direct object topicalization is preferred when the object is as high, and particularly when it is higher in animacy than the subject. That is, by the way, our rule of dative overriding, and that is the rule of "personal *a*". Why would dative overriding and "personal *a*" be the same rule? They both flag an atypical alignment of subject and direct object in Spanish. We repeat here the animacy alignments for convenience, and because the repetition serves as a summary of dative overriding:

(27) a.   [+H] , [-H] Typical alignment of <u>NOM</u>, **ACC** (<u>verber</u> and **verbed**)
        Atypical alignments:
  b.   [-H] , [+H] "personal *a*" + dative overriding in 22/22 Spanish-speaking countries
  c.   [+H] , [+H] "personal *a*" in 22/22 Spanish-speaking countries
        "personal *a*" + dialectal *leísmo* in León and Castilla (Spain), when the direct object is masculine, singular
  d.   [-H] , [-H]. "personal *a*" + inanimate dative overriding in 22/22 countries

3.8. An outline of a verber/verbed theory of case in English

All of the sentences with the dozen or so verbs in English whose only object must be an indirect object are intransitive.[30] All other sentences whose only object does not require a preposition are transitive. That is the outline of a <u>verber</u>/**verbed** theory of case marking in English in 35 words. The intransitive sentences whose only object must be an indirect object are verber-less but not subjectless. Those sentences have **verbed** and <u>verbee</u>. As the VVASP in Chapter 1 predicts, the **verbed** is the subject. When the verbed is the subject, any other object must be introduced by a preposition. If that prepositional object is an indirect object, it will always be a verbee: *appeal(1), appear, be, belong, cost, happen, matter, occur, remain, seem, sound(1).*[31] Sentence (28a) below comes from a careless headline reproduced in Bathroom Reader's Institute (2002). It is a play on words on the two *appeals* in English: the one that is used in intransitive sentences because it has **verbed** (**prostitutes**) and <u>verbee</u> (<u>Pope</u>), and the one that is transitive because it has <u>verber</u> (<u>prostitutes</u>) and **verbed (the new city ordinance)**.

(28) a. **Prostitutes** appeal <u>to Pope</u>. (Bathroom Reader headline)
(appeal 1)
   b. <u>Prostitutes</u> appeal **the new city ordinance**. (appeal 2)

Let us finish this chapter by thanking the reader for taking the time to read it.

(29) a. <u>I</u> give **thanks** <u>to you</u>!
   b. <u>I</u> thank <u>you</u>!
   c. Thank <u>you</u>!
   d. *Ich danke <u>Ihnen</u>*! (German)
      'I thank <u>you</u>'
   e. ¡(Yo) <u>Les</u>   doy **(las) gracias**!
      I   <u>you-pl-DAT</u> give (the) thanks
      'I give <u>you</u> **my thanks**!'
   f. ¡(Yo) <u>Les</u>   agradezco!
      I   <u>you-pl-DAT</u> thank
      '(I) thank <u>you</u>!'
   g. watashi-wa anata-ni   kanshasuru   (Japanese)
      I   <u>you-pl-DAT</u> thank
      'I thank you'

The object in (29d) is an indirect object, presumably because German *danke* 'to thank' has to be marked in the lexicon as an "inherent dative" (Van Valin & LaPolla 1997: 356).[32] Marking a verb as an "inherent dative" means that the grammar rules of the language do not have an explanation for why the object is indirect. Chapters 4 and 5 will show not only that *danke* does not have to be marked as an "inherent dative" verb, but that it appears that verbs do not have a script specifying whether they are transitive or intransitive, or whether the only object of this or that verb follows a general rule or has a script stipulating its lexical properties. If *danke* is *giving thanks* or *dar gracias*, as it is in English, in Spanish, in Japanese, and presumably in many other languages, that annotation in the lexicon is not needed in the grammar of German, as the explanation for accusative (direct object) and dative (indirect object) will show for English in Chapter 4 and for Spanish in Chapter 5.

There is evidence for this analysis of *danke* in "Mano a mano", a tango composed by Carlos Gardel, Esteban Flores, and José Razzano. The tango makes reference to having paid "**the favors** <u>to someone</u>":

(30) **Los favores recibidos** (yo) creo   habér<u>te</u>los   pagado.

The favors   receivedI   believe to have-you-DAT-them-ACC paid
'I believe I have paid you the favors I (have) received (from you)'

3.9. Conclusions

The solution to the transitivity paradox proposed in this chapter makes it possible to state that transitivity is BINARY, at least for Spanish and English. Such a characterization of transitivity was possible with the <u>verber</u> and **verbed** inferences, and with a rule of dative overriding, a rule for which strong evidence was shown in five languages belonging to three different families. The grammar of Spanish needs the same rule to account for "personal *a*". When we put together the animacy alignments in (27a-d), "personal *a*", and dative overriding, the connection is clear: *a* marks non <u>verber</u>, and an indirect object pronoun (*le/les*) distinguishes a <u>verbee</u> from a **verbed**. The stronger the need to distinguish the verbee from the verbed, the more necessary that indirect object pronoun is.

BINARY: consisting of two members, *0-1* (or *yes-no*). A sentence is transitive, or it is not. There are no degrees of transitivity in a sentence. A sentence is not more or less transitive. It is transitive if it has a verber and a verbed. It is intransitive if it has a verber or a verbed, but not both.

The <u>verber</u> and **verbed** inferences make easily understood by college students (and probably by younger ones) the powerful insights of the Unaccusative Hypothesis, one of the most influential discoveries in linguistic theory. An understanding of unaccusativity, reserved until now to linguists (due to the complexity of the issues and all of the "linguistese" needed to explain all of the terms) is now accessible to learners of any L2 and to native speakers. The awareness that the subject of one of the two possible main types of intransitive sentences is a **verbed** has the potential to enhance significantly the understanding and learning of second languages in college, and perhaps in high school. With a rule of dative overriding, case marking is more predictable than thought. Chapter 4 explores this issue in English; Chapter 5, in Spanish.

Notes

1 Comrie (1989: 128) stated this observation in terms of A (an agentive subject) and P (a direct object patient) as follows: "In other words, the most natural kind of transitive construction is one where the A is high in animacy and DEFINITENESS, and the P is lower in animacy and definiteness". Comrie (1989: 128) defines definiteness as, "the presupposition that the referent of a

definite noun phrase is identifiable by the hearer; in terms of English structure, a definite noun phrase will either be a pronoun, a proper name, or a common noun introduced by the definite article or a demonstrative or a preposed possessor". (The definite article in English is *the*). As Fillmore (1968: 55) observed, "If there is an A[gent] it becomes the subject". It is also uncontroversial that the direct object is overwhelmingly inanimate (and often indefinite), as observed by Givón (1979: 52), among many others.

2 Specialized or important terms will be capitalized the first time they are used, and when particularly relevant. They are explained when needed.

3 De Swart (2007) reports that in a study of one thousand simple transitive sentences in Norwegian, Øvrelid (2004) found that just over 2% of those sentences had an accusative higher in animacy than the nominative, and most of them were experiencers of sentences with a subject stimulus. (That is, they were sentences with verbs like *frighten*). Øvrelid also found that 90% of the accusatives were inanimate.

4 As in previous chapters, the <u>verber</u> is <u>underlined</u>; the **verbed, bold**; and the <u>ver-bee, double underlined</u>. In sentences like (1a), **a las estudiantes** is an underlying **verbed** and that is the reason for the **bold**. That **verbed** is "marked" as a dative, as the <u>les</u> suggests.

5 These alignments make it a lot easier to understand differential object marking (DOM). That issue is beyond the scope of this proposal.

6 To the best of my knowledge, Talmy (1985: 99–101) is one of the first scholars to discuss these patterns as stimulus-subject vs. experiencer-subject verbs. Other scholars refer to stimulus-subject vs. stimulus-object verbs.

7 It has also been invoked for the fifty or so verbs in Spanish like *gustar*, the verberless verbs in §5.3.

8 As §5.5 shows, some sentences with <u>verber</u> and <u>verbee</u> have a **verbed** that is omitted because it is easily RECOVERABLE. RECOVERABLE is a term in linguistics for an object that need not be in the sentence, but it is clear from context. For example, *I wrote <u>my Mom</u>* is a reduced version of *I wrote <u>my Mom</u> a letter*, in turn a version of *I wrote **a letter** <u>to my Mom</u>*.

9 Chapter 5 will discuss verbs in which there is a difference in meaning when its only object is marked with accusative or dative. Some of those verbs are *encantar, importar, aprovechar, pegar*. One *appeal* takes nominative and dative in English; the other, nominative and accusative, as sentences (28a,b) at the end of this chapter show. That is an example of an accusative/dative alternation with a difference in meaning. Those are two different verbs.

10 Abbreviations are as follows: ACC: accusative; DAT: dative; NOM: nominative; fem: feminine; masc: masculine; pl: plural; pro: pronoun; 1sg: first person; singular, 3sg: third person, singular.

11 Remember from Chapter 1 that the notation '#' means that the sentence is not an inference from the sentence at issue (Huddleston & Pullum 2002: 35).

12 A resultative sentence is a sentence that expresses a result: the chicken is defrosted; the veggies are washed; the oil is hot.

13 The order DAT, NOM (A las estudiantes les gustan los exámenes) is more frequent, and there is *no* difference in meaning. The relative frequency of each word order is an interesting issue for research. The frequency has to do with privileging animacy (which is what the marked – atypical – word order highlights), and it makes processing easier, as §5.3 suggests. Although Table 4.1 in Vázquez Rozas (2006) does not exactly represent this frequency, one can infer from her table that the frequency of a dative preceding its nominative is 78%

to 92%. This includes, of course, the DAT clitic without the full form. A more accurate count must factor in the distinction between dative overriding and true dative objects.

14 *Leísmo* will be explained in the following section, after example (16).

15 See endnote 1 for a definition of definiteness by Comrie (1989: 128). Observe also that the definite article entails that the referent of the noun that the speaker is using is identifiable by the listener. The definite article is associated with old (known) information. It also entails that *the+noun* is a totality. Observe:

(i) A tiger came into the room.
(ii) The tiger listened to the professor. (cf. *A tiger listened to the professor)

Tiger is new information in (i) but known information in (ii). Interestingly, *the room* and *the professor* are known information in the context in which a professor is using this example. Notice that *the tiger*, *the room*, and *the professor* are a totality: each of those phrases refers to all of the things in the world that they refer to (that room, that professor, and the tiger in the professor's example).

A proper name is more definite than a noun with a definite article. A proper name not only refers to the totality of someone called *Bernardo*; that *Bernardo* named by a speaker is a unique individual known by the speaker and their listener(s).

16 "[…] a tendency in the language to introduce in the 3rd person pronoun a gender difference: *le* for the masculine accusative, *la* for the feminine, *lo* for the neuter, to the detriment of the case difference. But this tendency does not reach its full development. The dative neuter *le* remains unchanged. The plural accusative *les* does not thrive as much as the singular *le*". (Translation by the author).

17 Thanks to Yasuko Takata Rallings for providing these examples (p.c. 2017).

18 La Paz and Santa Cruz are two cities in Bolivia.

19 "Marked" is the specialized term in linguistics. "Atypical" has been used because it is more intuitive.

20 With subject and direct object, it is unimaginable to think that the Unaccusative Hypothesis can be understood by college and high school students, and that they can use it to learn an L2.

21 There is a distinction in L2 learning between learning and acquisition. You learn through study and explicit instruction. I leave a definition of language acquisition to the acquisitionists.

22 "Accusative *a*" is a first level of DIFFERENTIAL OBJECT MARKING (DOM) that distinguishes the **verbed** from the verber. A dative clitic *le(s)* distinguishes a beneficiary from a **verbed**. Those are, roughly, two tiers of DOM in Spanish. The discussion of such an important issue is beyond the scope of this book.

23 Chapter 4 explores in detail case marking in English; Chapter 5 does so in Spanish.

24 The rule in textbooks for Spanish is that a human direct object requires *a* before it. Lapesa (1983: 99) writes that *a* is required if the direct object refers to *persona individuada* 'individuated person'. Remember that proper names are definite, and they require "personal *a*". More than individuated, that object requires differential object marking ('*a*') the more definite it is. See endnotes 1 and 15 for a definition (and examples) of definiteness.

25 Although with a different verb, I found an interesting example: *¿Cuál es el número que le antecede al que el 20 le precede?* https://es.answers.yahoo.com/question/index?qid=20070612110456AAyDAZ6 (Notice the use of *le*. That is dative marking). (Last accessed July 2020)

26 This was a quick web check. It would not be surprising to find out that the frequencies aligned with the order a,b,c, at least for some verbs. This is an invitation to others to look into this issue.

27 An inanimate direct object does not accept *a* when there is no doubt as to which is the verber and which is the verbed.

> (i) El huracán   destruyó veinte   casas.
> 'The hurricane destroyed twenty houses'
> (ii)*El huracán   destruyó a veinte   casas.
> 'The hurricane destroyed to twenty houses'

28 See glosses in (19) above.

29 "Personal *a*" is also the rule when one of the participants is singular and the other plural, a case in which ambiguity should not arise. The need to avoid ambiguity (the traditional explanation in traditional Spanish grammar – repetition intended) cannot be invoked to explain differential object marking. On the other hand, an atypical animacy alignment explains the occurrence of differential object marking.

> (i) Los críticos elogiaron a Penélope. (Critics praised Penélope).

30 Remember that for a sentence to be transitive, one of its participants has to be marked with the accusative, and this necessarily implies that there is another participant marked with the nominative case. (This is known as Burzio's Generalization). Tina Fey[NOM] rocked **the boat**[ACC] is transitive; **The boat** rocked[NOM] is intransitive.

31 The notation '*appeal*(1)' and '*appeal*(2)' means that there are two *appeal* verbs in English. One is transitive and the other is intransitive, as shown in (28). The same goes for *sound*(1) and *sound*(2). See Table 4.1 (Chapter 4).

32 Van Valin & LaPolla (1997: 355) state this stipulation in terms of M-intransitivity for the German verb *helfen*, which presumably assigns only one macrorole, and this must be stipulated in the lexical entry for the verb. The point here is that the stipulation is not needed, neither in terms of macrorole nor in terms of "inherent dative", as it would be stated in other frameworks. It is reasonable to assume that *helfen* and *danke* function the same way. They do function the same way in Spanish, as the examples in (29) show, and as the discussion of *ayudar* 'help' in §5.7 will show.

References

Bathroom Readers' Institute. 2002. *Uncle John's biggest ever bathroom reader*. San Diego: Thunder Bay Press.

Comrie, Bernard. 1989. *Language universals and linguistic typology*. 2nd ed. Chicago: University of Chicago Press.

De Swart, Peter. 2007. *Cross-linguistic variation in object marking*. Utrecht: LOT. (Doctoral dissertation.) Retrieved from (https://www.lotpublications.nl/Documents/168_fulltext.pdf) (Last accessed 2020).

Draye, Luk. 1996. The German dative. In Van Belle, William & Van Langendonck, Willy (eds.), *The dative. Vol 1: Descriptive studies*, 155–216. (Case and grammatical relations across languages). Amsterdam: John Benjamins.

Fernández Ramírez, Salvador. 1987. *Gramática española. El pronombre*. 2d ed. Vol. Prepared by José Polo. Madrid: Arco/libros, S.A.

Fillmore, Charles J. 1968. The case for case. In Bach, Emmon & Harms, Robert T. (eds.), *Universals of linguistic theory*, 1–88. New York: Holt, Rinehart and Winston. https://doi.org/10.1017/S0022226700002875.

Gil, David. 1982. Case marking, phonological size, and linear order. In Hopper, Paul & Thompson, Sandra A. (eds.), *Studies in transitivity. Syntax and semantics*, vol. 15, 117–141. New York: Academic Press.

Givón, Talmy. 1979. *On understanding grammar*. New York: Academic Press.

González, Luis H. 1997. *Transitivity and structural case marking in psych verbs. An HPSG fragment of a grammar of Spanish*. Davis: University of California. (Doctoral dissertation.)

Hopper, Paul & Thompson, Sandra A. 1980. Transitivity in grammar and discourse. *Language* 56. 251–295. (https://www.jstor.org/stable/413757).

Huddleston, Rodney & Pullum, Geoffrey K. 2002. *The Cambridge grammar of the English language*. Cambridge: Cambridge University Press.

Jespersen, Otto. 1905. *Growth and structure of the English language*. Leipzig: B. G. Teubner.

Lapesa, Rafael. 1983. *Historia de la lengua española*. 9th ed. Madrid: Espasa.

Øvrelid, Lydia. 2004. Disambiguation of grammatical functions in Norwegian: Modeling variation in word order interpretations conditioned by animacy and definiteness. In Karlsson, Fred (ed.), *Proceedings of the 20th Scandinavian Conference of Linguistics*. Helsinki, Finland: Department of General Linguistics, University of Helsinki.

RAE (Real Academia Española). 1973. *Esbozo de una nueva gramática de la lengua española*. 21st reprinting. Madrid: Espasa Calpe, S.A.

RAE (Real Academia Española y Asociación de Academias de la Lengua Española). 2010. *Nueva gramática de la lengua española. Manual*. Madrid: Espasa Libros S.L.U. (https://www.rae.es/obras-academicas/gramatica/manual-de-la-nueva-gramatica).

Talmy, Leonard. 1985. Lexicalization patterns. Semantic structure in lexical forms. In Shopen, Timothy (ed.), *Language typology and syntactic description. Vol. 3: Grammatical categories and the lexicon*, 57–149. Cambridge: Cambridge University Press.

Van Hoecke, Willy. 1996. The Latin dative. In Van Belle, William & Van Langendonck, Willy (eds.), *The dative. Vol 1: Descriptive studies*, 1–37. (Case and grammatical relations across languages). Amsterdam: John Benjamins.

Van Valin, Robert D., Jr. & Lapolla, Randy J. 1997. *Syntax: Structure, meaning and function*. Cambridge: Cambridge University Press.

Vázquez Rozas, Victoria. 2006. Gustar-type verbs. In Clements, Joseph Clancy & Yoon, Jiyoung (eds.), *Functional approaches to Spanish syntax*, 80–114. New York: Palgrave Macmillan. (https://pdfs.semanticscholar.org/49d3/117788a84917f086ae694f6ae482ff075fce.pdf?_ga=2.201348755.369220713.1597701565-1866771009.1594303638)

4 There are verberless sentences, but no subjectless ones

4.1. Introduction

Linguistics does not have a satisfactory answer for the question of how native speakers determine subject, direct object, and indirect object. Children "know" this implicitly by the time they begin Kindergarten, and obviously, those children have not had any grammar lessons. They probably know that you speak in words, and that those words are strung together in what they will find out later are called sentences. Sometimes, we speak in paragraphs. As teachers of a second language (L2), we try to get our students to move from talking in words and sentences to talking in paragraphs.

Those of us who have taught or learned an L2 know that distinguishing a direct from an indirect object in an L2 is at times a formidable challenge. The reader will remember that Davis (2001: 2) – and undoubtedly several others – wondered why subject and direct object are not reversed in countless sentences like *the hyenas approached the carcass, Len forgot the keys, the ranger suggested a hike along the coast, Terry owns a Toyota, the speculators rebuffed further inquiries into their finances and did not return phone calls*. That is clearly an admission that we, linguists, do not really know how subject and direct object work. Not even in English, a language in which position almost always gives it away. Is the subject the participant that comes before the verb? That is the case in the five variations of (1a) below. The notion of subject is hiding three functions with a clearly different meaning in the Sandra Bullock sentences:

(1) a. The Academy gave **an Oscar** to Sandra Bullock.
   b. The Academy gave Sandra Bullock **an Oscar**.
   c. **An Oscar** was given to Sandra Bullock by the Academy.
   d. **An Oscar** was given to Sandra Bullock.
   e. Sandra Bullock was given **an Oscar** by the Academy.
   f. Sandra Bullock was given **an Oscar**.

Instead of a direct object (an Oscar) and an indirect object (to Sandra Bullock) as in (1a), the sentence in (1b) has two "objects": a "primary" object (Sandra Bullock) and a "secondary" object (an Oscar). Observe that the order of the objects has to be reversed, and the preposition *to* (or *for*, depending on the verb) has to be omitted. Furthermore, (1b) is called the double object construction. In (1a), Sandra Bullock is an indirect object because she is introduced in the sentence by the preposition *to*, not because she is 'indirectly' affected from the giving of an Oscar to her, as claimed (for comparable sentences) in traditional Spanish grammar. Who or what is more affected (positively, in this case) from an event of giving the Oscars: the Oscar given to her or Sandra Bullock? If Sandra Bullock had not won an Oscar, she would have not made it into this book and would not have become famous as the actress in the Sandra Bullock sentences in *The Fundamentally Simple Logic of Language*. Joke aside, the direct object does not have to be affected to be a direct object. I admire and praise Tina Fey. Is she affected? Not at all. She does not know who I am, let alone that I admire her. I believe that the intuition behind the notion of direct object is that it is an object directly "governed" by the verb; that is, an object that the verb can take directly, without the mediation of a preposition. The indirect object in (1a) is introduced by a preposition. Interestingly, this explanation also applies to all objects introduced by other prepositions, aptly called prepositional objects.

In (1c-f), *an Oscar* and *Sandra Bullock* are the subject by position and by agreement: the participant before the verb is overwhelmingly the subject in English. Furthermore, *an Oscar* and *Sandra Bullock* agree with *was*, the corresponding form of the auxiliary verb *be* in the passive voice. Based on subject-verb agreement, we can say that *an Oscar* and *Sandra Bullock* are the subject by form. However, as these variations of this sentence show, subject and form are a moving target. Meaning, on the other hand, is constant. The <u>verber</u>, the **verbed**, and the <u>verbee</u> are constant, as shown throughout this book. They are constant and easily trackable, unlike subject, direct object, and indirect object, which are clearly neither constant nor easily trackable. Readers are invited to consider whether they remember the main point of sentences (5a,b) in Chapter 1, repeated below. Please do not read the next paragraph if you prefer to think about this for a moment.

(2)   a.   Julio worked.
       b.   Taxes increased.

The point was that when there is just one participant in a sentence, that participant is virtually always the subject. In terms of linguistics, that subject is marked with the nominative case. A sentence can have just one participant if it is grammatical with just one or if one of the two (or three) participants can be omitted. But that only participant can be the <u>verber</u> or the **verbed**, and that is a very important difference.

4.2. An outline of a <u>verber</u>/verbed theory of case in English[1]

All of the sentences with a dozen or so verbs in English whose only object must be an indirect object are intransitive. All other sentences whose only object does not require a preposition are transitive. That is an outline of a <u>verber</u>/**verbed** theory of case marking in English in 35 words. The intransitive sentences whose only object must be dative are verberless but not subjectless. Those sentences have **verbed** and <u>verbee</u>. As the VVASP predicts, the nominative (the subject) passes the **verbed** inference. The indirect object is a benefactee or malefactee: *appeal(1), appear, be, belong, cost, happen, matter, occur, remain, seem, sound(1)*. Example (3a) below comes from a careless headline reproduced in Bathroom Reader's Institute (2002). The reader is invited to see the point before proceeding with the explanation below.

(3) a. **Prostitutes** appeal <u>to Pope</u>. (Bathroom Reader headline)
         (appeal 1)
     b. <u>Prostitutes</u> appeal **the new city ordinance**. (appeal 2)

Sentence (3) is a play on words based on the two *appeals* in English: The one that is used in intransitive sentences because it has **verbed (prostitutes)** and <u>verbee</u> (<u>Pope</u>), and the one that is transitive because it has <u>verber</u> (<u>prostitutes</u>) and **verbed (the new city ordinance)**. **The new city ordinance** can be appealed by the prostitutes, but the Pope is not appealed by them.

Sentence (3b) also shows a powerful prediction regarding this explanation of case in English. Every only object that does not require *to* or *for* (or any other preposition) will pass the verbed inference; the subject of all of those sentences will pass the verber inference. Furthermore, our definition of intransitivity as a sentence with verber or verbed (but not both) accounts for sentences like those with verbs of activity (intransitive "action verbs") like *cry, snore, work, yawn*: the subject is the crier, snorer, worker, yawner, etc. It also accounts for unaccusative sentences with verbs like *arrive, die, fall, exist*, etc. The subject of those sentences will be the arrived, the dead, the fallen, the existed, etc.[2] It accounts as well for passive voice sentences (as in 1c-f above) and unaccusativizations as in *the door opened, the river froze, the tree branch broke*. Nothing has to be changed in this definition for it to account for the unaccusative verbs that have two participants often (or more often than not): *appeal* (1), *appear, belong, cost, happen, matter, occur, seem, remain*: they are verberless. The **verbed** unaccusativizes and the VERBEE is marked with the dative because it is a BENEFACTEE or MALEFACTEE. To my knowledge, Gil (1982) was the first scholar to refer to the only object of unaccusative verbs like those just listed as the benefactee or malefactee. We have used in previous chapters the term *VERBEE*, which captures the generalization over these two terms and the indirect object of verbs with three participants in English. Sandra Bullock is the awardee in (1) above, regardless of her grammatical function as indirect object, primary object, or subject. In more general terms, she is the verbee, a term that this coming section explains in detail.

4.3. There are verberless sentences, but there are no subjectless ones

Let us do a warm-up activity that will help the reader understand better the rest of this chapter. The task of the reader is to determine verber, **verbed**, and verbee, which will not be coded. The reader can take out pencil and paper (or do it mentally) before proceeding to the explanation. Curious readers might want to use markers to do this in color. There are two sentences in Italian and two in French.[3] The "recycling" is on purpose: the sentences that are familiar to the reader will help in distinguishing verber, **verbed**, and verbee in the unfamiliar ones. Some of the sentences will be explained below.

(4)   The Academy gave an Oscar to Sandra Bullock.
(5)   The Academy gave Sandra Bullock an Oscar.
(6)   Sandra Bullock was given an Oscar.
(7)   I sent Boston[i] a book to Boston[ii].
(8)   Francesca si è tagliata un dito.   (Italian)
(9)   Romeo amava Juliet.   (Italian)
(10) Celie a vu un film.   (French)
(11) Un nouveau film est sorti.   (French)
(12) We sent Grandma our children.
(13) This computer belongs to Tatiana.
(14) An accident happened to me.
(15) Small fonts give me a headache.
(16) This jerk gave me the finger.
(17) Pay attention to the details, won't you?
(18) Does a cup of coffee appeal to anyone?

(19) How does a cup of coffee sound to you?
(20) Prostitutes appeal to Pope.

In sentences (4–6), the Academy is the giver, an **Oscar** is the given, and Sandra Bullock is the benefactee. That is true not only for (4), but also for (5) and (6). Remember that if (4–6) are true, (21a) is true, but (21b) is not.

(21) a. An Oscar was given.
     b. #Sandra Bullock was given.   *What?*

Consider now (22). The reader is invited to stop reading and see whether they can discover what the two Bostons refer to.

Lastname   city
(22) I sent a book to Boston[i] to Boston[ii].

All readers will have realized that one of those two Bostons must be the city in Massachusetts, USA. Most speakers of English (and those with some knowledge of English or a gift for language) might have realized that the other Boston must be a last name. For sentence (22), the subscript [i] means that Boston[i] refers to one of them and Boston[ii] refers to the other. In linguistics, we would say that the referent for Boston[i] is different from the referent for Boston[ii]. My PhD adviser said once in class (some 35 years ago in 2020) that referent is what in the world a word refers to. A smart and funny explanation of referent. Boston[i] refers to one of the students I had a few years ago at the university where I teach. Boston[ii] is the city in Massachusetts, USA. Thus, in (22), I am the sender, the book the sent, and Boston[i] the sendee. Boston[ii] is an adverbial of place (a locative phrase). On the surface, and purely by form, *to Boston*[i] is identical to *to Boston*[ii], except, of course, for the subscript. Our coding will make this easier to understand and will help in deepening our understanding of this sentence in English, particularly for speakers of English as an L2.

(23) a. I sent **this book** to Boston[i] to Boston[ii].
     b. I sent Boston[i] **this book** to Boston[ii].
     c. *I sent Boston[ii] **this book** to Boston[i].
     d. #I sent Boston[i]. (cf. *I sent Boston[ii])

Sentence (23a) is a regular sentence in English with subject, direct object, indirect object (*to Boston*[i]), and with a locative phrase (*to Boston*[ii]). Sentence (23b) is the dative-shift version of (23a). The indirect object (the dative) is switched around with the direct object and must lose its *to* (or *for*).[4] In fact, the version with the "primary" object (the original indirect object) preceding the direct object in English is more frequent than the one in (23a). Two reasons come to mind. An object with fewer words tends to be closer to the verb than an object with more words. This rule is called in linguistics Heavy NP Shift, or simply, heaviness. If we think that the benefactee is often a person, and that many first names in English are often five PHONEMES or fewer, the probability that the benefactee is lighter than the verbed is very high.[5] I would have liked to have sent this manuscript to Ann, Beth, Carl, Dan, Ed, Fritz, Geoff, Ivan, Joan, etc. to get some feedback from them. (Those are names of famous linguists.) In addition, the benefactee is often just a pronoun. Indirect object pronouns in English have two or three phonemes (*me, you, her, him,* [*it*], *us, them*). By heaviness, that <u>benefactee</u> object will be predicted to precede the **verbed**. The other factor is animacy, which is, in a sense, hard to tell apart from that [+H] being lighter than the direct object, which is often [-H]. In a way, animacy and heaviness go naturally together in that order in English. The primary object is overwhelmingly lighter than the secondary one.

Let us return to our Boston sentences. Boston[i] can shift and precede the book, as (23b) shows. However, Boston[ii] cannot shift, as (23c) shows, even if the rest of the sentence would be grammatical without Boston[i]. As the reader can predict, nobody can send Boston[ii] anywhere. Although someone can send Boston[i] somewhere, (23d) is not true if (23a) is true. With this explanation, it is easy to understand why speakers do dative shift in *send the boarder a package* but not in #*send the border a package*, a famous example from Bresnan (1978). Now we know not only that speakers of English do not say the version with *border* but also why: *border* is a locative but *boarder* is a <u>benefactee</u>. Native speakers of English can readily *send the boarder a package* thanks to the strength of the intuition of the <u>verbee</u>.

Let us see how different Boston[i] and Boston[ii] can be:

1. Can I send Boston[i] somewhere?
2. Can I send Boston[ii] anywhere?
3. What happens to Boston[i], if *I send Boston[i]a book*?
4. What happens to Boston[i] if *I send Boston[i]to Ireland*?
5. What happens to Boston[ii] if *I send Boston[ii]to Ireland*?
6. Is Boston[i] the sent in (3)?
7. Is Boston[i] the sent in (4)?
8. To Boston[i] = to Boston[ii] in FORM (except for the subindex). Are they the same in MEANING, or are they different?

Here are the answers. Do not look if you would like to discover the answers for yourself.

1. Yes. To a conference, to another office, to the grocery store, to Ireland, etc.
2. No.
3. She gets the book.
4. Boston[i] goes to Ireland.
5. That will be impossible.
6. No. The sent is the book. She is the sendee (verbee).
7. Yes.
8. Very different. To Boston[i] is a beneficiary. If I send her a book, she will get the book. To Boston[ii] is a location. If I send Boston[i] a book to Boston[ii], Boston[i] will get a book; Boston[ii] will not. Speakers of English know intuitively that *I sent Boston[i] a book to the city of Boston[ii]* is a possible sentence in English, but *I sent the city of Boston[ii] a book to Boston[i]* is not.

Let us return to the question of distinguishing verbed from <u>verbee</u>. If we sent Grandma our children (as in 12 above), which of the following two inferences is correct?

(24) a. The sent were our children.
    b. The sent was Grandma.

The entailment in (24a) is correct. We did not send *Grandma* anywhere. *Grandma* is the primary object in this sentence. *Grandma* is the benefactee. In (12), *our children* is the secondary object, which means that they are really the direct object. Thus, when we unshift the sentence in (12), as in (25b) below, *our children* is expressed immediately after the verb; *Grandma* is expressed after *our children*, and it must have *to*.

(25) a. We sent <u>Grandma</u> **our children**. (=12)
    b. We sent **our children** <u>to Grandma</u>.

[handwritten annotation: Our children: verbed / Grandma: verbee]

Readers who are not sure about the rest of the sentences in (8–20) will be able to do them after the following exercises and the short explanations. The reader is invited to determine who/what is the verber, the verbed, and the verbee in the following sentences. There will be two participants. One of the slots will be empty. Readers who can do this right away have understood very well. Some readers might not always be sure. That is expected. They will be able to do the exercises if they try again after they finish reading this chapter. Remember, one of the slots will remain empty.

(26) a. Tatiana owns this computer.
    b. owner: _Tatiana_
    c. owned: _computer_
    d. ownee: _____

(27) a. This computer belongs to Tatiana → _passive voice_
    b. belonger: X
    c. belonged: _Computer_
    d. belongee: _Tatiana_

(28) a. I caused an accident.
    b. causer: _I_
    c. caused: _an accident_
    d. causee: X

(29) a. An accident happened to me.
    b. happener: X
    c. happened: _Accident_
    d. happenee: _Me_

Tatiana is the owner and this computer is the owned. Why? Because of the logical inferences (entailments) that anyone can draw from this sentence: if it is true that Tatiana owns this computer, it is also true that Tatiana is the owner, and that this computer is the owned (because this computer is owned by Tatiana). There is no ownee in this sentence. With *belong*, what is Tatiana? Is she the belonger? If that were the case, English speakers could say that *Tatiana belongs this computer*. She is not the belonger. Is the computer the belonger? If this computer were the belonger, speakers of English would say sentences like *this computer belongs Tatiana*. There is no belonger. Thus, one is going to be the belonged and the other the belongee. The reader should stop reading and think which is which. Who/what can aptly be called the belongee? The belongee would be the benefactee, who/which can be an owner because the concept of the indirect object had its origin to refer to the participant in the sentence who receives a gift, and therefore owns it. That concept extended to ownership (or loss of it). If Tatiana is the benefactee (because she was given a computer or because she bought it), she is predicted to be the owner. If this computer belongs to Tatiana, she is the owner. In fact, *this computer belongs to Tatiana* entails that Tatiana is the owner. Then, the computer must be the belonged. If this is still somewhat hard to see, it is not because it is difficult but more because it is new. I trust that readers who are not convinced yet will see it with other examples. We have followed a very simple but rigorous logic. Every claim in this book is based on what the data show, without the need for any theoretical constructs.[6] It might take several examples to understand that verbs like *appeal, appear, belong, be, cost, happen, matter, occur, remain, seem* are verberless but not subjectless. In the absence of a verber in a sentence, the verbed becomes the subject. The verbee of these verbs will always be introduced by the preposition *to*. In short, these verbs will have verbed and verbee. Indeed, the reader will remember that the VVASP (8 in Chapter 1) predicts that in the absence of a verber, the verbed is the subject. I wanted to leave this last prediction for the end because I anticipated that some readers would have made the connection before they reached this point. In other words, the VVASP predicts that the subject of verberless sentences is the verbed. That prediction is, of course, correct.

The sentence with *cause* in (28) is uncontroversial. I was the causer; the accident, the caused. Passive voice is a very reliable test for direct objecthood. If I caused an accident, an accident was caused by me. What about *happen*? Do we have a happener? If we had a happener, the sentence in English would be *I happened an accident*. Nobody says that. Now the reader should understand why we can say that the accident is the happened. I have never heard or read the string of words a "happened accident", but my language intuition leads me to believe that it should be OK. Moving on, who is the happenee? If an accident happened to me, the prediction is that I was the malefactee. When someone is in an accident, and that accident is their fault, it is true that they *had* an accident, and that they *own* that accident, because their insurance will have to pay for the damages to the other party.[7] Again, the VVASP predicts that the accident will be the subject.

4.4. A sentence with a mandatory direct object and an indirect object in English. Or, an insult turned into a teaching moment

One beautiful spring morning in March of 2015, I was driving to work. I was at a stop light, and I must have gotten a little distracted. I looked through my rear view mirror and saw the driver in the car behind me giving me the finger. The light was now green. It was probably not the first time that I had been given the finger, but it was the first time that I had seen it. It did not bother me. I simply drove away. Within seconds, I realized that precisely on that day, two hours later, I was going to be teaching indirect objects in Spanish, a tough lesson for speakers of English. It was the perfect example: one of the very few sentences in English with a mandatory direct and indirect object. This is rather remarkable because English is a language with very few indirect objects compared to other languages in the world. Consider these sentences:

(30) a.   This jerk gave me the finger.
    b.   %This jerk gave the finger to me.
    c.   #This jerk gave me.
    d.   #This jerk gave the finger.

Everyone knows (30a). (30b) is very infrequent. Bresnan & Nikitina (2008) show that although infrequent, it has been used in authentic texts; that is, in writing by native speakers. The reader knows that both (30c) and (30d) look grammatical on the surface, but neither is entailed by (30a). No speaker of English utters sentences like those. (30d) could be a sentence in English, but with two conditions. First, *the finger* must be changed to *a finger*. It is very unlikely for someone to have just one finger (the finger), and even more unlikely that such a person would decide to give it to someone else, for a transplant, for example. Thus, perhaps the only plausible interpretation of (30d) would be a situation in which someone gave their only finger to someone else, so that other person could have a finger transplant. I have never heard or read about a finger transplant. If the jerk who gave me the finger were to give someone else his only finger so that the person could have a finger transplant, I would stop calling him a jerk, and would call him instead "the sweet finger-donating guy". Now the reader understands why I wrote that *give someone the finger* is a sentence with a mandatory indirect object in English. It is actually a mandatory double object construction, but we already know that the double object construction is a variation (an alternation, a more specialized term in linguistics) of a sentence with a direct and an indirect object.

There is a song in English (a hit at its time!) called *It don't matter to me*. That title is very revealing. The writer of that song failed to do subject-verb agreement, but he did not fail to mark *me* as a <u>verbee</u>.[8] I wrote that there are about a dozen verbs in English that have two participants, but those two participants are not a verber and a verbed. One of those participants is a verbed and the other the verbee. The verbee is the participant introduced by *to*, and it is overwhelmingly human. The verbed can also be human, but it is almost always non human. That verbee is a benefactee or a malefactee. The reader is invited to think about the following verbs as the verbed, verbee takers. Furthermore, the reader should think how the verbee gets something (or has it)[9] or loses it.

(31) Appeal(1), appear, belong, be, cost, happen, matter, occur, remain, seem, sound(1)

If something appears to you, you have an opinion of that something. Likewise for *seem*. If an idea occurs to you, you have an idea. An idea came to you, which is not a contradiction of this explanation because the idea is the verbed and you are the owner of that idea. People are born because they are bore by their mother (the bearer); but perhaps for language economy, we often leave the mother out of the picture. Conceivably, for a reason similar to that of referring to our wedding day as the day in which *we* (*were*) *married*; hardly ever as *so and so married my wife and me*. The marrier (a judge, a pastor, a priest) is often irrelevant. Not that one's Mom is irrelevant. It is simple economy: I was born in the last millennium is enough for practical purposes. There is no need to say that my mother gave birth to me in the last millennium.

Incidentally, and at least for Spanish, pedagogical and textbook grammars often explain that *gustar* is equivalent to *X is pleasing to you*. That explanation is incorrect. The *to* is there because of *is*, not because of *please*. *Please* takes pleaser and pleased in English. I am very pleased to have been able to bring *The Fundamentally Simple Logic of Language* to the speakers of many languages. *Be* always requires a dative (an indirect object introduced by *to* or *for*) if the benefactee or malefactee is expressed in the sentence: *how a printer works is astonishing to me, fall weather is amazing to many people, testing predictions is exciting to scientists*, etc. *Gustar* verbs work in Spanish like the verbs in (31) work in English. More generally, *gustar* verbs work like verberless verbs in the grammar of the learner.

4.5. Simplifying linking by one third: indirect objects need not be part of argument realization

Some readers might remember the observation that linguistics did not have a satisfactory answer for the question of how speakers determine subject and direct object in their native language. Teachers, linguists, and other scholars who know or work on languages might be wondering why this author left out indirect object in that question. After all, distinguishing direct from indirect object is very likely a more difficult task (as we will see) than that of distinguishing subject and direct object. It is definitely a very challenging task in a second language.

That task is about to become easier, though. In most sentences with a direct object and a prepositional object, the indirect object is easily omissible, but the direct object is not. Consider (32a-n):[10]

(32) a. My children and I load hay onto wagons for a living.
    b. My children and I load wagons with hay for a living.
    c. My children and I load hay for a living.
    d. My children and I load wagons for a living.
    e. *My children and I load onto wagons for a living.

f.   *My children and I load with hay for a living.
g.   I sent this manuscript to Sam in December.
h.   I sent this manuscript in December.
i.   #I sent Sam in December.
j.   I sent Sam this manuscript in December.
k.   I baked a cake for Rosie.
l.   I baked a cake.
m. I baked Rosie a cake.
n.   #I baked Rosie.

We have six objects with a preposition: *onto the wagon, with hay, for a living, in December, to Sam, for Rosie*. The last two introduce indirect objects in English. With this omission test, they behave as the other four prepositional objects: they cannot be in the sentence if the direct object is not; however, they do not have to be there. Most (di)transitive sentences are grammatical with just a direct object. In a sense, the indirect object is omissible, as virtually any other prepositional object is in a sentence that also has a direct object.

We can now ask a very important question: do we need to account for the indirect object in a theory of who does what (to whom) in a sentence, the main task of linguistics? Davis (2001: 119) suggested an answer for this question: "In general, arguments realized as objects of PPs don't necessarily need to be present in a verb's lexical semantic representation, because prepositions can add their own semantic contribution". ARGUMENT is the specialized word in linguistics (and philosophy) for participants in a sentence. A PP is a prepositional phrase; that is, a phrase with a preposition (*onto, with, for, in, to, for*, etc.) followed by its object, which is more often than not a noun. A LEXICAL SEMANTIC REPRESENTATION is a representation of the features (characteristics) that define a word. Presumably, the lexical semantic representation of a verb will include information as to whether the verb is transitive or intransitive, and what kind of subject and object it will take. As if every verb had a script for the instructions on how to use it. It appears to this author that this is not the way languages work. Chapter 6 will briefly take up this point.

Returning to the answer by Davis, prepositional objects, including the indirect object, which is introduced in English by *to* or *for*, need not be part of linking (the decision as to who does what (to whom) in a sentence). Speakers arrive at the meaning of *onto the wagon, with hay, for a living, in December, to Sam, for Rosie* COMPOSITIONALLY by putting together the meaning of each of its parts in these sentences and in any sentence in which they are found. A prepositional object is never a subject or a direct object, the two core or nuclear participants in a sentence. The meaning of every productive prepositional object is completely predictable from its parts, and so is its meaning contribution to any sentence. Their meaning is so predictable, that the benefactee will always be the so-called primary object in English, the participant that can unshift, and the one that cannot pass the verbed inference because it is the dative (the indirect object).

The strength of the intuition of the dative (the indirect object) explains why speakers of English do dative shift with *boarder* but not with *border* in *send the boarder a package* vs. **send the border a package* (*the boarder* is a benefactee who receives the package; (to) *the border* is a locative that cannot receive a package). More generally, it explains why speakers can drop *to* and *for* when they introduce an indirect object: because it is always clear who is doing what to whom, as semantic roles were informally defined a few decades ago.[11] A primary object analysis as the basic pattern (vis-à-vis a prepositional indirect object analysis) in English (and in other languages, according to Dryer 1986) is hard to maintain after the evidence adduced in this proposal. The primary object cannot be the basic object in English because it is readily omissible and does not pass the verbed inference, whereas the secondary object does pass it. In addition, the primary object is a benefactee/malefactee that can unshift, and then will require *to* or *for*. Without exception.

This is a good time to remind the reader why we need to distinguish subject and direct object. We can also answer the question asked by Davis (2001: 2) when he wondered why subject and direct object cannot be reversed in countless sentences. If I say that I like **Sally**, we all agree that I am the <u>liker</u> and **she** is the <u>liked</u>. She might not even know that I like **her**. However, if I were to say that <u>Sally</u> likes **me**, that is a totally different situation. If the last sentence is true, then it is also true that **I** am liked by her.

Finally, this section has shown that at least in Spanish and English, a theory of assigning subject, direct object, and indirect object can be simplified by removing the last function. Thus, if any object introduced by a preposition (*onto the wagon, with hay, for Rosie, in December*) need not be part of linking because speakers know the meaning and function of that prepositional phrase by computing the meaning of each part, a theory of linking has to account just for subject and direct object. We proposed our VVASP in Chapter 1. Let us repeat it here for convenience as (33):

(33) Verber/Verbed Argument Selection Principle (VVASP)

> The <u>verber</u> is always the subject of the sentence. The **verbed** is the direct object of a transitive sentence or the subject of an intransitive or an intransitivized one.

Readers know now that the verber is the participant that passes the verber inference; the verbed, the participant that passes the verbed inference.

4.6. From Hopper & Thompson, Tsunoda, and Malchukov to Burzio. Or, how transitivity is not only discrete; it is binary

The best characterization of transitivity is probably that of Burzio (1986: 178), known as Burzio's generalization: "All and only the verbs that can assign a θ-role to the subject can assign accusative Case to an object".[12] The VVASP is consistent with his generalization. However, when the object of verbs like *asustar* is indirect, those sentences are not transitive, if transitivity is defined in terms of Case (accusative), if we follow Burzio's Generalization. Our characterization of a transitive sentence as one that has verber and verbed covers those sentences, as the explanation of the transitivity paradox showed in Chapter 3. Chapter 3 showed plenty of evidence for the proposal of dative overriding. With the alternation of verbee/verbed explained, we have a clearer picture of nominative, accusative, and dative. Notice that if we "test" the 11 verberless verbs (*appeal(1)*, *appear*, *be*, *belong*, *cost*, *happen*, *matter*, *occur*, *remain*, *seem*, *sound(1)*) with Burzio's generalization, these are the results: those verbs do not have a verber. One of the participants must be a verbed, and in the absence of a verber, that participant must undergo mandatory unaccusativization; therefore, it must be expressed as the subject of the sentence. The other participant is always marked with dative. By virtue of being a dative, that participant is predicted to be overwhelmingly human, and to be a benefactee or malefactee. All of those predictions are correct.

Having accounted for the dative marking of the equivalent in Spanish of verbs like *frighten*; and having shown also that they are transitive (as they are in English), we have shown that transitivity is in the sentence, and that it is binary. A sentence is transitive or it is intransitive, although many transitive verbs can be used intransitively. Therefore, the present proposal is simpler than the ten parameters of transitivity in Hopper & Thompson (1980). A re-thinking of the parameters in a hierarchy as in Tsunoda (1985; 2015) and Malchukov (2005; 2015) is a step in the right direction, but it is far from being simpler and more predictive than this proposal. A detailed comparison with those proposals is beyond the scope of a proposal advanced for the first time.

Since the dative of sentences with the dozen or so verberless verbs in English requires a preposition to mark the object of those verbs, that dative need not be part of a theory of assignment of subject and direct object, if we agree with the observation by Davis (2001: 119) that objects with a preposition need not be part of linking. The indirect object of any sentence with three participants also requires *to* or *for* in English. Once we have accounted for the dozen or so verberless verbs, the VVASP predicts that for all other SENTENCES in English with two participants and whose only object is not introduced by a preposition, one of the participants will satisfy the verber inference, and it will be the subject; the other participant will satisfy the verbed inference, and it will be the direct object. And each of those sentences will be transitive. This one-paragraph outline of transitivity in English is a better understanding of this phenomenon than that of many linguists. In addition, it should be understood by many L2 learners of English.

Be and *cost* appear to behave somewhat different from the other verberless verbs. A brief discussion of them follows.

(34) This shirt cost me ten dollars.

Since *me* is a benefactee (*this shirt belongs to me*) and *ten dollars* appears to be a direct object because this sentence could unshift and be expressed as (35a), linguists might ask why (35b) is not a sentence in English:[13]

(35) a.   This shirt cost ten dollars to me.
     b.   *Ten dollars were cost by this shirt.

The VVASP can answer this question. *Ten dollars* is an ADJUNCT; it is not really a direct object. *This shirt* is the cost (the verbed) and *me* is the benefactee. If I am the benefactee, I should be the owner of the shirt. I am. If the shirt were the "coster", English would have a sentence like *this shirt cost me*; if I were the "coster", English would have a sentence like *I cost this shirt*. Neither is a sentence in English. For those skeptical of this analysis, here is a related one.

(36) a.   Cristina buys ten pounds of rice for ten dollars.
     b.   Ten dollars buy ten pounds of rice.
     c.   Cristina opens this door with a wooden key.
     d.   A wooden key opens this door.

The promotion of an instrument (a wooden key) to verber is something that was clearly established by Fillmore (1968: 43), if not before. In an event of buying, *ten dollars* is very comparable to an instrument. An instrument somewhat more abstract, but an instrument nonetheless. Observe these other examples:

(37) a.   The boxer weighed in at 140 pounds.
     b.   *140 pounds were weighed in at by the boxer.

    c. This room measures 150 sq. ft.
    d. *150 sq. ft. are measured by this room.

Ten dollars is an adjunct in (34) above, as are *140 pounds* and *150 sq. ft.* Could *the boxer* be the weighed in and *the room* the measured? If so, they should be able to passivize. Then those sentences are missing a verber that can be left out. That is also true. A medical examiner and a home appraiser are possible subjects for these sentences. The passive voice for each sentence is as follows:

(38) a. The boxer was weighed in by a medical examiner.
      b. This room was measured by a home appraiser.

There sure are many other observations. But the evidence for this proposal should suffice for now. The following table summarizes the discussion so far, which has focused on explaining CASE in English, particularly dative case in sentences with two participants. It is in these sentences where dative really shows up in English. Readers will find a few comments about *come* and *be* below.

Table 4.1 Verbed/verbee vs. verber/verbed verbs

	Unaccusative (verberless) verbs in English	Corresponding transitive verb	
Appeal(1)	Does **skating** appeal <u>to you</u>?	<u>The defendant</u> appealed **the decision**.	Appeal(2)
Appear	**A ghost** appeared <u>to me</u>.	<u>The magician</u> showed **a rabbit**.	Show
Arrive	There arrived **a package** <u>for you</u>.	<u>The mailperson</u> brought **a package**.	Bring
Be	**Semantics** is so interesting <u>to me</u>!	<u>Semantics</u> interests **me**.	Interest
Belong	**We** belong <u>to the earth</u>.	<u>We</u> do not own **the earth**.	Own
Come	**An idea** came <u>to me</u>.	<u>They</u> brought **new ideas**.	Bring
Cost	**This watch** cost <u>me</u> 200 dollars.	<u>They</u> charged <u>me</u> **200 dollars** (for this watch).	Charge
Happen	Did **an accident** happen <u>to you</u>?	<u>The fog</u> caused **an accident**.	Cause
Matter	**Honesty** matters <u>to good citizens</u>.	Do <u>you</u> mind **a question**?	Mind
Occur	**An idea** occurred <u>to her</u>.	Did <u>they</u> give you **that idea**?	Give
Remain	**Two weeks** remain <u>to you</u>.	<u>We</u> left **the project** for next week.	Leave
Seem	**It** seems <u>to me</u> **that you are on the right track**.	<u>I</u> suppose **that you are on the right track**.	Suppose
Sound (1)	**A frappucino** sounds good <u>to me</u>.	<u>They</u> sounded **the alarm**.	Sound(2)

Intuitively, some of these verbs are somewhat common with two participants. Particularly if one compares them with *die, fall*, and *exist*, for example. In fact, the promise to comment on *come* and *be* is due to the fact that *come* and *arrive* appear to contradict what I have just written about these verbs often having two participants. *The mail arrived, the energy bill came* are very frequent sentences with just the **verbed**. Perhaps because we would say that *an idea occurred to us*, we do not say very often that *an idea came to us*. Although as I write this, I realize that we would say that *an idea came our way* but not that **an idea occurred our way*. When we respond, "it doesn't matter", the indirect object *to me* is as implicit as the direct object *some food* when one says that one has already eaten.

Be is interesting to linguists for several reasons. It does not take a direct object in English or in Spanish. Being a copular verb, it probably does not take a direct object in any language. *Be* behaves like *appear* and *seem* in the sense that the three verbs can take an adjective. That adjective is often followed by a dative object in both languages.

(39) a. Copular verbs are interesting <u>to linguists</u>. (39a = 39b).
    b. <u>A los lingüistas</u> <u>les</u> son interesantes los verbos copulativos.
      'To linguists, copular verbs are interesting'.
    c. <u>A los lingüistas</u> <u>les</u> parecen interesantes los verbos copulativos.
      'Copular verbs seem interesting to linguists'.
    d. Distinguishing the vowels in English is difficult <u>for learners of English as an L2</u>.
    e. <u>A los aprendices del inglés como segunda lengua</u> <u>les</u> es difícil distinguir las vocales del inglés.
    f. Distinguir las vocales del inglés <u>les</u> es difícil <u>a los aprendices del inglés como segunda lengua</u>.

Sentence (39b) seems a little forced. The reason is that the best verb in this case would be *parecer* 'seem', as in (39c). (39d) and (39e) are a little long. It was the first example that came to mind. I wanted to keep it. The reader will observe that the version in Spanish is "upside down". That is the preferred order in Spanish, although the other order is possible. This ordering preference will be briefly explained in §5.3. In the meantime, a simple rule suffices: in verberless sentences, the verbee tends to precede the verbed in Spanish.

4.7. Everything is connected

We have shown that sentences like <u>The Academy</u> gave <u>Sandra Bullock</u> **an Oscar** is a variation of <u>The Academy</u> gave **an Oscar** <u>to Sandra Bullock</u>. The *to* is marking the indirect object in this sentence. In a sentence like I baked Rosie **a cake**, we all know that the baked was the cake, not Rosie. That is a sentence in English because we also say that I baked **a cake** for Rosie. By meaning, Rosie is the benefactee in both sentences. We do not engage in baking people. The *for* is marking the indirect object in this sentence as well. Thus, indirect object need not be part of LINKING or ARGUMENT STRUCTURE, (the part of linguistics that has to determine who is doing what in a sentence). That *for* is there in every sentence – visible or not – but always recoverable, in sentences with verber, **verbed**, and verbee. Likewise, the *to* is also there – visible or not – for sentences with verber, **verbed**, and verbee. The *to* is also there, and always visible, for the verbee of verberless sentences, because those sentences are grammatical with just their **verbed**, as when one can simply say that **an accident** happened. However, when there is a second participant in those verberless sentences, that participant always requires *to* to introduce the benefactee or malefactee: ***an accident*** *can happen to anyone.*

4.8. Conclusions

As stated in Chapter 1, a sentence is transitive if it has a verber and a **verbed**. This statement seems trivial in English, but it is clearly not trivial in many languages in which that **verbed** (a direct object) is expressed in the sentence as if it were an indirect object. Those "false" indirect objects behave like direct objects, but no true indirect object behaves like a direct object.[14] That was the transitivity paradox explained in Chapter 3, and that is the underlying thinking in the theory of CASE marking (assignment of nominative or accusative) outlined in this chapter. Verber and **verbed** show that the subject of an intransitive sentence is not necessarily the participant doing something (the verber); the subject is often the **verbed**. The same way that Roberto is the worker but **taxes** are the **increased**, as shown in sentences (5a,b) in Chapter 1, if I say that I told you, *you* is the tellee because the told is **what** I told you. With verber and **verbed**, it will be easier to teach to L2 learners of English why *I told you* is very different from *I told on you.*

The distinction between verber and **verbed** allowed us to explain auxiliary selection in languages with a *have/be* distinction, to understand reflexive constructions better than before, to solve the transitivity paradox, to understand "personal *a*" and *leísmo* in Spanish as the same rule, and to propose an intuitive and LEARNABLE theory of transitivity: a sentence is transitive if it has a verber and a **verbed**. The verber/**verbed** also led us to identify the verberless sentences in English; that is, the sentences with verbs like *appeal, appear, belong,* etc. CASE marking is a lot more predictable than thought.

Now we can better understand the language paradox in Chapter 1. How can children tell apart subject, direct object, and indirect object by age seven, yet these notions are so hard to understand and apply in an L2? Telling apart subject, direct object, and indirect object is a perplexing paradox for any L2 learner working with nominative, accusative, and dative because nominative/accusative and accusative/dative have been inextricably tangled for 22 centuries. On the other hand, the child does not really have to distinguish the indirect object from the direct object. The former is introduced by a preposition or is trackable (thanks to the fact that it does not pass the **verbed** inference) when shifted around with the direct object. It is always the benefactee or malefactee; that is, the verbee. For the distinction involving subject and direct object, children work with verber and verbed, two basic inferences mastered implicitly by age seven. In fact, children from languages with a *have/be* distinction begin to use the latter with a non verber subject soon after age two (Snyder & Hyams 2015).

Notes

1 The repetition of this paragraph is on purpose. A few readers have confirmed that they find the "second pass" useful in order to better grasp the point.
2 Notice that "the existed" sounds unnatural. It is because *exist* is a state (as opposed to an activity, like *run*; an accomplishment, like *learn a definition of transitivity*; and an achievement, like *pop a balloon*).
3 We have explained some of these sentences. Some learners benefit from some repetition. It is great if the reader can do the exercises right away. It is fine if some sentences require some thinking or review.
4 Remember that the sentence *I baked **a cake** for Sam* is synonymous with *I baked Sam **a cake***.
5 A phoneme is a sound in the language that when changed in a word, causes a difference in meaning. The words *bake, cake, fake, Jake, lake, make, nake, rake, take, wake* start with a different phoneme in English.
6 Observe what happens in the following sentences when there is a pause before *seriously*:

  (i) If I cannot support a claim with an example, I will not say it seriously.
  (ii) If I cannot support a claim with an example, I will not say it; seriously.

7 Two interesting questions come to mind. Why do speakers of English not say sentences like *an accident was happened?* or, *I was happened?* With the verber and verbed inferences, many L2 teachers or college students can answer those questions. Before, only a linguist who knows well the Unaccusative Hypothesis could do so.
8 David Gates is the composer. The song was released in 1969.
9 If *a alguien se le quiebra **un brazo*** (if someone breaks his/her arm) that is expressed with an indirect object in "heavy indirect object using languages". In English, *you break your arm*. *Your* codes the inalienable possession. Languages with robust dative use an indefinite article with parts of the body with verbs like

break. The owner of that inalienable body part is the verbee. An amputee is a person who had **a limb** (or several) amputated.

10 The verbs *put* and *place* come to mind as one exception. Another provocative issue for research.

(i) I put the deodorant in the drawer.
(ii) *I put the deodorant. (cf. I put deodorant on)

A few verbs allow the omission of an "easily recoverable" direct object, as when someone writes (to) their parents. Some of those verbs will be discussed in §5.4.

11 This statement is often repeated. I asked Stan Whitley (p.c. 2018), who uses this statement repeatedly in his writing. He said that he might have been the one who came up with this wording.

12 Burzio's Generalization states in somewhat formal terms the traditional intuition that a transitive sentence is a sentence with subject and direct object. Burzio added the theta role (θ-role) piece. Theta roles were proposed in 1965.

13 Perlmutter & Postal (1983: 91–92) discuss sentences similar to these.

14 As discussed in this chapter, the city of Boston has not been sent anywhere (as in 23c), nobody is going to bake Rosie (as in 32n), and Sandra Bullock will not be given to anyone (as in 1e,f).

References

Bathroom Readers' Institute. 2002. *Uncle John's biggest ever bathroom reader*. San Diego: Thunder Bay Press.

Bresnan, Joan. 1978. A realistic transformational grammar. In Halle, Morris & Bresnan, Joan & Miller, George A. (eds.), *Linguistic theory and psychological reality*, 1–59. Cambridge: The MIT Press.

Bresnan, Joan & Nikitina, Tatiana. 2008. The gradience of the dative alternation. In Uyechi, Linda & We, Lian Hee (eds.), *Reality exploration and discovery: Pattern interaction in language and life*, 161–184. Stanford: Center for the Study of Language and Information.

Burzio, Luigi. 1986. *Italian syntax: A government-binding approach*. Dordrecht: Reidel.

Davis, Anthony R. 2001. *Linking by types in the hierarchical lexicon*. Stanford: Center for the Study of Language and Information.

Fillmore, Charles J. 1968. The case for case. In Bach, Emmon & Harms, Robert T. (eds.), *Universals of linguistic theory*, 1–90. New York: Holt, Rinehart & Winston.

Gil, David. 1982. Case marking, phonological size, and linear order. In Hopper, Paul & Thompson, Sandra A. (eds.), *Studies in transitivity. Syntax and semantics*, vol. 15, 117–141. New York: Academic Press.

Hopper, Paul & Thompson, Sandra A. 1980. Transitivity in grammar and discourse. *Language* 56. 251–295.

Malchukov, Andrej. 2005. Case pattern splits, verb types, and construction competition. In Amberber, Mengistu & de Hoop, Helen (eds.), *Competition and variation in natural languages: The case for case*, 73–117. Amsterdam: Elsevier.

Malchukov, Andrej. 2015. Valency classes and alternations: Parameters of variation. In Malchukov, Andrej & Comrie, Bernard (eds.), *Valency classes in the world's languages. Vol 1: Introducing the framework, and case studies from Africa and Eurasia*, 73–130. Berlin: De Gruyter. https://doi.org/10.1515/9783110338812.

Perlmutter, David M. & Postal, Paul M. 1983. The 1-advancement exclusiveness law. In Perlmutter, David M. & Rosen, Carol G. (eds.), *Studies in relational grammar*, vol. 2, 81–125. Chicago: The University of Chicago Press. (https://press.uchicago.edu/ucp/books/book/chicago/S/bo3620141.html). (This link takes to vol. 1. Vol 2 shows up only in Amazon.com).

Snyder, William & Hyams, Nina. 2015. Minimality effects in children's passives. In Di Domenico, Elisa & Hamann, Cornelia & Matteini, Simona (eds.), *Structures, strategies and beyond: Essays in honour of Adriana Belletti. Vol. 223: Linguistik Aktuell/Linguistics today*, 343–368. Amsterdam: John Benjamins. https://doi.org/10.1075/la.223.

Tsunoda, Tasaku. 1985. Remarks on transitivity. *Journal of Linguistics* 21. 385–396. https://doi.org/10.1017/S0022226700010318.

Tsunoda, Tasaku. 2015. The hierarchy of two-place predicates: Its limitations and uses. In Malchukov, Andrej & Comrie, Bernard (eds.), *Valency classes in the world's languages. Vol 2: Case studies from Austronesia and the Pacific, the Americas, and theoretical outlook*, 1597–1625. Berlin: De Gruyter. https://doi.org/10.1515/9783110338812

5 The case for the true *gustar* (*piacere*) verbs in Spanish

5.1. Introduction

This chapter shows that sentences with a [+H] only object are transitive, even if that only object "looks like" an "indirect object", if that object passes the verbed inference. That includes verbs like *asustar* 'frighten', *aburrir* 'bore', *molestar* 'bother', *preocupar* 'worry', *sorprender* 'surprise', etc. Those verbs are not truly *gustar* (verberless) verbs, like the ones discussed in section 5.3. This section (5.3) turns the obligatoriness of a pronoun duplicating a **verbed** or a <u>verbee</u> when that **verbed**/<u>verbee</u> is preverbal into a reliable test in Spanish for *gustar* (verberless) sentences. This test is a reliable indicator of the true *gustar* verbs (*piacere* verbs in Italian, verbs like *belong* and *matter* in English). Section 5.4 offers motivation for an indirect object preceding a subject with verbs like *gustar*: if the subject is determinerless, it is acceptable after the verb but ungrammatical before it. This is a very desirable interaction among word order, unaccusativity, and the Naked Noun Constraint proposed in Suñer (1982). Section 5.5 adds to the evidence to explain dative and accusative objects. It is particularly relevant to highlight the contribution of a clitic doubling an indirect object: it shows that said object is indirect (a verbee) because the direct object can be omitted. The doubling clitic *les* in *les servimos a los invitados* 'we served [food to] our guests' helps in processing the sentence as the invited folks being the benefactees. No need to mention that they were served *food* (*les servimos comida a los invitados*). Without a dative clitic, *servimos a los invitados* invites an interpretation in which that dinner is not one to which an attentive reader might want to be invited. Section 5.6 discusses a few verbs in which a single direct object or indirect object does express a difference in meaning. Those verbs have verbee and verbed when the only object is dative; they have verber and verbed when the only object is accusative. They are verbs in Spanish similar to pairs like *matter/mind*, *belong/own*, *seem/suppose* in English. Section 5.7 shows that *ayudar* 'help' is *darle ayuda a alguien* 'give help to someone', which is more often than not expressed as *ayudarle a alguien* 'help someone[dative]'. The explanation proposed accounts for the dative clitic with *ayudar* (*le ayuda al papá* 'helps her father'). The same explanation accounts for the dative in *helfen* 'help' in German and the verb corresponding to *thank* (give thanks) in German, Japanese, Spanish, and presumably in some other languages.

5.2. "Indirect objects" that pass the verbed test are verbeds, not <u>verbees</u>

Remember from Chapter 4 that a sentence like (1a) is transitive, even when the object seems to be indirect as in (1b,c), because it allows the inferences in (1d-g). Sentence (1f) is infrequent in Spanish with verbs that express states (NON ACTIONAL situations, like owning a house or liking the sound of the sea). Sentence (1e) is a more frequent way of unaccusativizing (expressing the accusative or direct object as the subject) in Spanish, perhaps because it better portrays an event (an ACTIONAL situation), something which is easier to see when the verb is in the preterite, as (1h) shows:[1]

> ACTIONAL VERBS: The term "actional" is used in Snyder & Hyams (2015) to refer to activities (*run, sneeze, snore, swim*), accomplishments (*build a chair, memorize a song*), or achievements (*pop a balloon, find your keys*). Non actional verbs are states; that is, verbs which express situations in which the verber is not necessarily doing anything (owning a house, believing in decency, loving your family).

(1) a. Los exámenes preocupan **a las estudiantes**.
   b. Los exámenes (**les**) preocupan **a las estudiantes**.[2]
   c. **A las estudiantes** <u>les</u> preocupan <u>los exámenes</u>. (Direct object topicalization)
   d. **A las estudiantes** las preocupan <u>los exámenes</u>. (Direct object topicalization)
   e. **Las estudiantes** <u>se</u> preocupan con/por (= a causa de) los exámenes. (Unaccusativization)
   f. %**Las estudiantes** son preocupadas por los exámenes. (Passive = unaccusativization)
   g. **Las estudiantes** están preocupadas. (Resultative sentence)
   h. **Las estudiantes** <u>se</u> preocuparon con/por (= a causa de) los exámenes. (Unaccusativization)

Preocupar 'worry', 'preoccupy' is the equivalent in Spanish of Italian *pre-occupare*.[3] It behaves in Spanish like any transitive verb, except that the object is more often than not marked as an indirect object. The preference for expressing that object as an indirect object instead of a direct object is explained with dative overriding. As Chapter 3 showed, the *preocupar* class (the class [or classes] of verbs whose only object is [+H]) is not really needed as a different class (at least in Spanish), once the <u>verbee</u>/**verbed** alternation is explained with dative overriding.[4]

On the other hand, the sentences in (2a,c) are intransitive. *Gustar* is the equivalent in Spanish of *piacere*, the prototypical verberless verb in Italian; that is, a verb without a <u>verber</u>. The reader knows now that the *piacere* (= *gustar*) verbs in English are those in Chapter 4, Table 5.1 (*appeal, appear, belong, matter, happen, seem*, etc.). In terms of this proposal, *gustar* is verberless, but not subjectless. Unaccusative or verberless verbs have **verbed** and <u>verbee</u>. In the absence of a verber, the **verbed** unaccusativizes (is "promoted" to subject), and the <u>verbee</u> is always marked as an indirect object, whether it appears in the sentence after the verb, as in (2a), or before it, as in (2c). Sentence (2b) is ungrammatical without *les* but is grammatical with *les* (as 2a shows).

(2) a. **Los exámenes** <u>les</u> gustan <u>a las estudiantes</u>.
   b. *Los exámenes gustan a las estudiantes.
   c. <u>A las estudiantes</u> <u>les</u> gustan **los exámenes**.
   d. *A las estudiantes las gustan los exámenes.
   e. *Las estudiantes se gustan.
   f. *Las estudiantes son gustadas.
   g. *Las estudiantes están gustadas.

Table 5.1 Preocupar *has* <u>verber</u>, **verbed**; gustar *has* **verbed**, <u>verbee</u>

<u>Verber</u>, verbed (Sentence 1)	Verbed, <u>verbee</u> (sentence 2)
a. <u>Los exámenes</u> (<u>les</u>) preocupan **a las estudiantes**.	a. **Los exámenes** <u>les</u> gustan <u>a las estudiantes</u>.
b. <u>Los exámenes</u> preocupan **a las estudiantes**.	b. *Los exámenes gustan a las estudiantes.
c. **A las estudiantes** <u>les</u> preocupan <u>los exámenes</u>.	c. <u>A las estudiantes</u> <u>les</u> gustan **los exámenes**.
d. **A las estudiantes las** preocupan <u>los exámenes.</u>	d. *A las estudiantes las gustan los exámenes.
e. **Las estudiantes** <u>se</u> preocupan.	e. *Las estudiantes se gustan.
f. % **Las estudiantes** son preocupadas.	f. *Las estudiantes son gustadas.
g. **Las estudiantes** están preocupadas.	g. *Las estudiantes están gustadas.

In Spanish, it is uncontroversial that *a las estudiantes* is an indirect object in (2a) due to the requirement of an indirect object pronoun (*les*) duplicating the object (*a las estudiantes*) when the object is indirect, even if it is postverbal. (2b) is ungrammatical without a pronoun duplicating the verbee. (2c) is grammatical because a verbee can be topicalized (expressed in preverbal position) if it is duplicated with the pronoun corresponding to a verbee. (2d) is ungrammatical because the duplicating pronoun is the one for a **verbed**, but *a las estudiantes* is a <u>verbee</u>. (2e-g) would be grammatical if *a las estudiantes* were the **verbed**. Table 5.1 shows sentences (1a-g) and (2a-g) side by side.

Sentences (3) and (4) provide equivalents in English of sentences (1) and (2). We will use the verberless verb *happen* for *gustar*, since *like* in English (like a few other verbs) shifted from intransitive (having verbed and verbee) to transitive (having verber and verbed) over 500 years ago (Jespersen 1924: 160).

(3) a. <u>Tests</u> worry **students**.
     b. *<u>Tests</u> worry to students.
     c. *<u>To students</u> worry <u>tests</u>.   (Direct object topicalization)
     d. *<u>Students</u> worry <u>tests</u>.
     e. *<u>Students</u> themselves worry.   (Unaccusativization)
     f. Students worry themselves.
     g. **Students** are/get/become worried by/with tests.   (Passive = unaccusativization)
     h. **Students** are worried.   (Resultative sentence)

(4) a. **Accidents** happen <u>to students</u>.
     b. *<u>Students</u> themselves happen.
     c. *<u>Students</u> are/were happened.   (Passive voice = unaccusativization)
     d. *<u>Students</u> are happened.   (Resultative sentence)

Since sentences with verberless verbs do not have a <u>verber</u>, the **verbed** unaccusativizes and is expressed as the subject of the sentence, as predicted by the VVASP (if there is no <u>verber</u>, the **verbed** is expressed as the subject). A true <u>verbee</u> will be marked with *a* and doubled with *le(s)* when it is a third person. The pronoun system of Spanish distinguishes direct object pronouns from indirect objects only in third person. The form for *you* formal is *usted* (often abbreviated as *Ud.* in writing), and it is the same as the one for third person.

The obligatoriness of a pronoun duplicating a **verbed** or a <u>verbee</u> when that **verbed** or <u>verbee</u> is preverbal can be turned into a reliable test in Spanish for verberless verbs. Since that object cannot be but an indirect

Table 5.2 Direct and indirect object pronouns in Spanish

	Subject pronoun	Direct object	Indirect object
I	yo	me	me
you (informal)	tú	te	te
you (formal)	usted	lo/la	le
he	él	lo (le)	le
she	ella	la	le
we	nosotros/nosotras	nos	nos
you (informal)	vosotros/vosotras	os	os
you (formal)	ustedes	los	les
they	ellos/ellas	los/las	les

object when the sentence is intransitive, only an indirect object pronoun can appear with it. Thus, the test is that if an object is truly indirect, the sentence will be grammatical only with an indirect object pronoun, and the referent for that indirect object is predicted to be a <u>benefactee</u> or <u>malefactee</u>; never a **verbed**.[5] Thus, we have a morphological test (*le/les*) coupled with a meaning test (benefactee/malefactee). When the sentence is grammatical with a direct object pronoun as well, that means that the sentence is transitive, the object is the **verbed**, and the option to use an indirect object pronoun is the result of dative overriding. If that object is a verbed, it will accept some (perhaps most) of the alternations in (1b-h). The more kinetic the verb (more "action-like"), the more alternations it will accept.

As Chapter 1 showed, <u>verber</u> is a generalization over buyer, cleaner, ignorer, mover, reader, understander, washer, writer.[6] Chapter 2 showed (at least implicitly) that <u>verbee</u> is a generalization over *recipient, goal, source, experiencer*, and more generally over *benefactee* and *malefactee*. We will make that point explicit in the following paragraph and in the following section.

Since the dative (the case of the indirect object) indicates the recipient of a gift, then the referent of the indirect object is the <u>benefactee</u> and owner (or <u>malefactee</u> and loser). The *recipient* or the *goal* is a possessor/benefactee. If someone experiences an emotion, s/he owns (has) that emotion: *fear, love, marvel, amazement, sadness, happiness*. If *an accident happens to someone*, they own that accident in the sense that those who are at fault have to pay for the damages (through their insurance). Both parties in the accident are clearly malefactees. If *an idea occurs to someone*, that is her/his idea. When *something matters to you*, you hold (= own) an opinion on the issue. If *something seems to you*, you own that perception or opinion; it is your perception or opinion. If *a shirt cost you 50 dollars*, you own it, and you are the benefactee for having acquired it. If *children were born to my wife and me*, they are the born, my wife was the bearer, and they are our

Table 5.3 Verbee /**verbed** vs. verber/**verbed** verbs in Spanish

✝	Unaccusative (verberless) verbs in Spanish	Corresponding transitive verb	
Atraer Attract, like (Appeal(1))	¿A usted le atrae **el patinaje?** ¿A usted le gusta **el patinaje?**	El acusado apeló **la decisión.**	Apelar (Appeal(2))
Aparecer	(Se me) apareció **un fantasma.**	El mago mostró **un conejo.**	Mostrar
Llegar	A usted le llegó **un paquete.**	El cartero/a trajo **un paquete.**	Traer
Ser	¡La semántica me es tan interesante! (La semántica es muy interesante para mí.)	%La semántica interesa **a Juana.** (cf. Juana se interesa en/por la semántica; Juana está interesada.)	Interesar
Pertenecer	Nosotros le pertenecemos a la tierra.	Nosotros no poseemos **la tierra.**	Poseer
Venir	Se me vino **una idea.**	Ellas trajeron **nuevas ideas.**	Traer
Costar	**Este reloj** me costó 200 dólares.	(Ellas) Me cobraron 200 dólares. (Por este reloj.)	Cobrar
Ocurrir	¿Te ocurrió **un accidente?**	La neblina causó **un accidente.**	Causar
Importar (1) (matter)	**La honestidad** les importa a los buenos ciudadanos.	Importan **flores** de Holanda.	Importar (2) (import)
Ocurrir	A ella se le ocurrió **una idea.**	¿Ellas te dieron **esa idea?**	Dar
Quedar (remain)	A Ud. le quedan **dos semanas.**	Dejamos **el proyecto** para la próxima semana.	Dejar (leave)
Parecer	Me parece (a mí) **que estás en la pista correcta.**	Supongo **que estás en la pista correcta.**	Suponer
Sonar(1)	Me suena bien **un frapuchino.**	Sonaron (tocaron) **la alarma.** (Hicieron sonar **la alarma.)**	Sonar(2)

children. If something causes my hand to burn, itch, or hurt, then *MY hand burns, itches, hurts.* Those familiar with the robustness of indirect object in Spanish, and with the fact that the determiner (*the, a, some, four*) for parts of the body (and clothing) is usually the definite article (because the [inalienable] possession is coded somewhere in the phrase), will now understand better why that possession is not shown with a possessive adjective: it is already encoded in the indirect object. That is exactly what Spanish does: *me arde/pica/duele la mano* 'my hand burns, itches, hurts', with *me* being an indirect object pronoun. There is no indirect object in English in *my hand burns, itches, hurts* or in *a machine dries **my** shirts*. Therefore, the possession must be encoded with the possessive adjective.

5.3. The true *gustar* (verberless) verbs in Spanish[7]

The verbs in (1–56) below are the verberless verbs in Spanish that I have been compiling for 25 years. There are some pairs similar to English *appeal* in the sense that the verb is transitive with one meaning and intransitive with another (see Tables 5.4 to 5.6 below). *Importar* 'import' is one of those verbs. When it is transitive, it means to buy goods from another country. The buying country is the importer and the goods are the imported. When it is intransitive, it means *matter*.[8] The issue is the **mattered** and the person to whom it matters is the _matteree_. If this were the first time that readers saw a noun like _matteree_, some readers might think that I am making up words. However, I trust that readers have seen _happenee_ and _belongee_ in

Table 5.4 Encantatarias/**encantado** vs. encantador/**encantadas**

Verbee, verbedEncantar(1): like a lot; love	Verber, verbedEncantar: cast a spell over; bewitch
a. **El helado** les encantó a las niñas.	a. El mago encantó **a las niñas.**
b. A las niñas les encantó **el helado.**	b.
c. *A las niñas las encantó **el helado.**	c. **A las niñas las** encantó el mago.
d. *El helado fue encantado.	d. **Las niñas** fueron encantadas (por el mago)
e. *El helado se encantó.	e. **Las niñas** se encantaron.
f. *El helado está encantado.	f. **Las niñas** están encantadas.

Table 5.5 The verb *aprovechar*: 'be of benefit to someone' vs. 'take advantage of'

Verbee, verbed	Verber, verbed
a. A las niñas les aprovechó **la medicina.**	a. Las niñas aprovecharon **la medicina.**
b. *Las niñas fueron aprovechadas.	b. **La medicina** fue aprovechada por las niñas.
c. **La medicina** les aprovechó a las niñas.	c. **La medicina la** aprovecharon las niñas.
d. *La medicina aprovechó a las niñas.	
e. *A las niñas las aprovechó la medicina.	d. **La medicina** se aprovechó.
f. *La medicina las aprovechó a las niñas.	

Table 5.6 Translation for the sentences in Table 5.5

Verbee, verbed	_Verber,_ verbed
a. <u>A las niñas</u> <u>les</u> aprovechó **la medicina**. To the girls, the medicine benefited.	a. <u>Las niñas</u> aprovecharon **la medicina**. The girls took advantage of the medicine.
b. *Las niñas fueron aprovechadas. *The girls were benefited.	
c. **La medicina** <u>les</u> aprovechó <u>a las niñas</u>. The medicine benefited the girls; the medicine caused the girls to feel well.	b. **La medicina** fue aprovechada por las niñas. The medicine was taken advantage of by the girls.
c. *La medicina aprovechó a las niñas. The medicine took advantage of the girls.	c. **La medicina la** aprovecharon <u>las niñas</u>. The medicine, the girls took advantage of it.
d. *A las niñas las aprovechó la medicina. *The girls, the medicine took advantage of them.	
e. *La medicina las aprovechó a las niñas. 'The medicine, it took advantage of the girls'.	d. **La medicina** <u>se</u> aprovechó. The medicine was taken advantage of.

the preceding chapter, and some will admit right away that _matteree_ is a legitimate word in English. Although this might be the first time that many readers have read or heard _matteree_, they are invited to associate the person with the _benefactee_ or _malefactee_ in what matters or not. *If **something** matters _to you_*, you hold or have an opinion about it. Readers who do not see clearly the _benefactee_ in _matteree_ are invited to consider how a _malefactee_ is easier to see if you are the _happenee_ in an accident. The accident is the **happened**, and those to whom it happened are the _happenees_. If *happen* had verber, English would have sentences similar to **an accident happened me*. The possession implied with most indirect objects should make it now clear to the reader that if ***this book*** belongs _to them_, they are the owner of this book. If ***this book*** belongs _to you_, **the book** is the **belonged** and _you_ are the _belongee_. If you are the _belongee_, you are, without any doubt, the owner.

    The only object in each of the examples that follow are all <u>verbees</u> of _verberless sentences_, except for eight.[9] In the following sentences, the string **_la_ verb NP** means that the verb is verberless and the pronoun must be _le_ (for a singular object).[10] I have left five sentences in which that string is grammatical (because the verb has verber and verbed, and *le* is the result of dative overriding) as an exercise for native speakers and advanced learners of Spanish as an L2, who should be able to discover some of those verbs. There are also three verbs with verber, verbed, and verbee. Since those verbs are not verberless, they are not really like *gustar*. There is a good chance that readers whose language has robust dative (like Spanish) will also be able to spot some of the 5+3 sentences with verber and verbed.

Those verbs will be revealed at the end of this section. A few representative verbs with verbed and verbee will be discussed in §5.6.

(5) a. <u>A Juana</u>   <u>le</u>   gustaron **las manzanas**.
       To Juana-DAT DAT-pro liked   the apples-NOM.[11]
       'Juana liked the apples'
     b. *A Juana   la   gustaron las manzanas.
       To Juana-ACC ACC-pro liked   the apples-NOM.

For the following examples, we will do numbers from 1 to 56 for ease of reference. The first five sentences will be fully glossed. The rest of the sentences will simply be translated.

---

(1) A Juana   le   aconteció una desgracia. (cf. *La aconteció una desgracia.)
     To Juana-DAT DAT-pro happened a disgrace-NOM
     'A disgrace happened to Juana'.
(2) A Juana   le   agradó el café. (cf. *La agradó el café.)
     To Juana-DAT DAT-pro pleased the coffee-NOM
     'The coffee pleased Juana'.
(3) A Juana   le   ajustó el vestido. (cf. *La ajustó el vestido.)
     To Juana-DAT DAT-pro fit   the dress-NOM
     'The dress fit Juana'.
(4) A Juana   le   apetece un café. (cf. *La apetece un café.)
     To Juana-DAT DAT-pro appeals a   coffee-NOM
     'A cup of coffee appeals to Juana'; 'Juana feels like having a cup of coffee'; 'a cup of coffee sounds good to Juana'.
(5) A Juana   le   ardió una mano. (cf. *La ardió una mano.)
     To Juana-DAT DAT-pro burned the hand-NOM
     'Juana's hand was burning'; 'Juana felt a burning in her hand'.
(6) A Juana le atañe la decencia. (cf. *La atañe la decencia.)
     'Decency concerns Juana'; 'Juana is concerned with decency'.
(7) A Juana le asustó un fantasma. (cf. *La asustó un fantasma.)
     'A ghost frightened Juana'.
(8) A Juana le basta una sonrisa. (cf. *La basta una sonrisa.)
     'A smile is enough for Juana'.
(9) A Juana le brillaron los ojos. (cf. *La brillaron los ojos.)
     'Juana's eyes sparkled'.

(10) A Juana le caben los libros en la mochila. (cf. *La caben los libros en la mochila.)
   'Juana's books fit in her backpack'.
(11) A Juana le cansan las caminatas por la playa. (cf. *La cansan las caminatas por la playa.)
   'Walks on the beach are tiring to Juana'.
(12) A Juana le cayó una piedra. (cf. *La cayó una piedra.)
   'A stone fell on Juana'.
(13) A Juana le causó sorpresa mi actitud. (cf. *La causó sorpresa mi actitud.)
   'Juana found my attitude surprising'; 'my attitude caused surprise in Juana'.
(14) A Juana le compete esa responsabilidad. (cf.*La compete esa responsabilidad.)
   'That is one of Juana's responsibilities'; 'that responsibility is in Juana's realm'.
(15) A Juana le convino la propuesta. (cf. *La convino la propuesta.)
   'That proposal suited Juana well'.
(16) A Juana le corresponde una tercera parte. (cf. *La corresponde una tercera parte.)
   'One third goes to Juana'; 'one third corresponds to Juana'; 'one third is for Juana'.
(17) A Juana le costó 40 *pesos* esa blusa. (cf. *La costó 40 *pesos*.)
   'That blouse cost Juana 40 *pesos*'.
(18) A Juana le creció el bigote. (cf. *La creció el bigote.)
   'Juana's mustache grew'; 'Juana's mustache grew on her'.
(19) A Juana le dolieron los pies. (cf. *La dolieron los pies.)
   'Juana's feet hurt'.
(20) A Juana le duró un día la fiebre. (cf. *La duró un día la fiebre.)
   'Juana's fever lasted one day'.
(21) A Juana le es útil la ley. (cf. *La es útil la ley.)[12]
   'Law is useful to Juana'.
(22) A Juana le fascina el helado. (cf. *La fascina el helado.)
   'Juana is fascinated with ice cream'; 'ice cream fascinates Juana'.
(23) A Juana le importaron los problemas. (cf. *La importaron los problemas.)
   'The problems mattered to Juana'.
(24) A Juana le incumbe ese escándalo. (cf. *La incumbe ese escándalo.)
   'That scandal is Juana's responsibility'.
(25) A Juana le faltaron tres dólares. (cf. *La faltaron tres dólares.)
   'Juana lacked three dollars'; 'Juana was three dollars short'.

(26) A Juana le gustaron las naranjas. (cf. *La gustaron las naranjas.)
     'Juana liked the oranges'.

(27) A Juana le latía el corazón. (cf. *La latía el corazón.)
     'Juana's heart was beating'.

(28) A Juana le llegó una carta. (cf. *La llegó una carta.)
     'A letter arrived for Juana'.

(29) A Juana le preocuparon las noticias. (cf. *La preocuparon las noticias.)
     'The news worried Juana'.

(30) A Juana le nació un hijo/a. (cf. *La nació un hijo/a.)
     'A child was born to Juana'; 'Juana gave birth to a child'.

(31) A Juana le ocasionó disgusto la noticia. (cf. *La ocasionó disgusto la
     noticia.)
     'The news caused displeasure to Juana'.

(32) A Juana le ocurrió un accidente. (cf. *La ocurrió un accidente.)
     'An accident occurred/happened to Juana'.

(33) A Juana le pasó una desgracia. (cf. *La pasó una desgracia.)
     'Something disgraceful happened to Juana'.

(34) A Juana le pareció bien la idea. (cf. *La pareció bien la idea.)
     'The idea seemed fine to Juana'.

(35) A Juana le pertenece esta casa. (cf. *La pertenece esta casa.)
     'This house belongs to Juana'.

(36) A Juana le pesa la patria. (cf. *La pesa la patria.)
     'Her country hurts to Juana'.

(37) A Juana le picó una mano. (cf. *La picó una mano.)
     'Juana's hand was itching'.

(38) A Juana le produjo sorpresa mi actitud. (cf. *La produjo sorpresa mi
     actitud.)
     'My attitude surprised Juana'.

(39) A Juana le quedó bien el vestido. (cf. *La quedó bien el vestido.)
     'The dress fit Juana well'.

(40) A Juana le repugna la corrupción. (cf. *La repugna la corrupción.)
     'Corruption is repulsive to Juana'.

(41) A Juana le resultó complicada la tarea. (cf. *La resultó complicada la
     tarea.)
     'The task turned out complicated for Juana'.

(42) A Juana le rindió el tiempo. (cf. *La rindió el tiempo.)
     'Juana's time (efforts) resulted in a good yield'. (Juana got a lot
     done in the time she had.)

(43) A Juana le salió un lunar. (cf. *La salió un lunar.)
     'A mole appeared to Juana'.

(44) A Juana le sangra la nariz. (cf. *La sangra la nariz.)
     'Juana's nose is bleeding'.

(45) A Juana le sirvió el vestido. (cf. *La sirvió el vestido.)
    'Juana's dress fit her well'.
(46) A Juana le sobraron tres horas. (cf. *La sobraron tres horas.)
    'Juana had three hours left'.
(47) A Juana le sorprendió mi actitud. (cf. *La sorprendió mi actitud.)
    'My attitude surprised Juana'.
(48) A Juana le sonó la idea. (cf. *La sonó la idea.)
    'The idea sounded fine to Ana'.
(49) A Juana le sucedió una desgracia. (cf. *La sucedió una desgracia.)
    'Something disgraceful happened to Juana'.
(50) A Juana le surgió un problema. (cf. *La surgió un problema.)
    'A problem arose for Juana'.
(51) A Juana le temblaron las manos. (cf. *La temblaron las manos.)
    'Juana's hands were shaking'.
(52) A Juana le tocó el turno. (cf. *La tocó el turno.)
    'It was Juana's turn'; 'Juana's turn was up'.
(53) A Juana le valió 40 dólares el vestido. (cf. *La valió 40 dólares el
    vestido.)
    'The dress cost 40 dollars to Juana'.
(54) A Juana le vino una cuenta. (cf. *La vino una cuenta.)
    'There arrived a bill for Juana'.
(55) A Juana le vino una idea. Se le vino una idea a la cabeza. Se le ocurrió
    una idea. (cf. *La vino una idea. *Se la vino una idea a la cabeza. *Se
    la ocurrió una idea.)
    'An idea came to Juana'; 'an idea occurred to Juana'.
(56) A Juana le zumbó una mosca. (cf. *La zumbó un mosca.)
    'A fly was buzzing around Juana'.

The total is 56. A few of them (*appear*, *arrive*, *come*) are verbs of movement. The verbs of movement are surely a few dozen, not just half a dozen
or so. That is an issue for further research. The verb *be* might be a special
case too; perhaps the unaccusativizer par excellence.

Readers with a good knowledge of Spanish and English will be able
to infer from the preceding list that the verberless verbs in English are
about one fourth of the preceding verbs (approximately 12 out of 48).
Determining how close in number and meaning the verberless verbs of
different languages are is an interesting issue for research. This issue was
researched during the 1980s by scholars, particularly by researchers working on Relational Grammar, but they were using grammatical relations, not
the verber/**verbed** inferences.

Table 5.3 above in § 5.2 is a translation into Spanish of the verberless
verbs in English in Table 4.1 (Chapter 4).

The verbs in (1–56) that are transitive and accept the pronoun *la* are: *asustar* 'frighten', *cansar* 'tire', *fascinar* 'fascinate', *preocupar* 'worry, preoccupy', *sorprender* 'surprise'. *Causar, ocasionar,* and *producir* are also transitive (<u>Mi actitud</u> <u>le</u> causó/ocasionó/produjo **sorpresa** <u>a Juana</u>).

5.4. Word order, verberless sentences, and the Naked Noun Constraint

The preferred word order for *gustar* sentences in Spanish is for the <u>verbee</u> to precede the **verbed**. Since languages seem to privilege [+H] referents, and <u>verbees</u> are overwhelmingly [+H], that [+H] tends to appear in preverbal position, particularly when the **verbed** (nominative) is [-H], which is the most frequent alignment of animacy and subject and object for these verbs. In other words, the alignment [-H]**verbed**, [+H]<u>verbee</u> is often expressed in a sentence as [+H]<u>verbee</u>, [-H]**verbed**. The preposition that introduces a <u>verbee</u> (*a*), and the duplicating pronoun that must occur when the object (direct or indirect) is preverbal, are two signals to the listener or reader that the preverbal participant is a non verber.

There is, in fact, a related and powerful factor at play. When the **verbed** is a naked common noun (a noun without an article or expression of quantity, as *cosas* 'things' below), the order <u>verbee</u>, **verbed** is mandatory due to the Naked Noun Constraint (NNC).[13] Consider this sentence from Alsina (1996: 117):

Numbering resumes after 5, and after the (1–56) set of verberless verbs.

(6)   A Margarita siempre le   pasan   cosas.
      To Margarita always   DAT-pro happen things.
      'Things happen to Margarita all the time'.

If we wanted to reverse the order in (6), we would end up with a violation of the NNC:

(7)   *Cosas siempre le pasan a Margarita.

The NNC amounts to a requirement for a preverbal common noun to be preceded by an article, a demonstrative adjective, or by an expression of quantity (*many* things). Since the benefactee/malefactee tends to be preceded by a definite article (or is more often than not a proper name), we can add DEFINITENESS to the factors favoring a <u>verbee</u>, **verbed** word order. (The other factor is animacy.) Remember from Chapter 1 that Comrie (1989: 128) defines definiteness as:

The presupposition that the referent of a definite noun phrase is identifiable by the hearer; in terms of English structure, a definite noun phrase will either be a pronoun, a proper name, or a common noun introduced by the definite article or a demonstrative or a preposed possessor.

(The definite article in English is *the*).

5.5. Indefinite object deletion

The square brackets in (8) below show a verbed that is often omitted. Such a deletion has been called indefinite object deletion (Heath 1976: 203; Mittwoch 1982; among many others). This structure is very PRODUCTIVE, not only in transitive predicates (as when Cecilia and David tell us that *they ate dinner* or that *they ate*; *they write novels* or *they write*, *they read detective novels* or *they read*, etc.), but also with ditransitive predicates, as the examples in (8) below show:

PRODUCTIVE: A phenomenon is more productive the more it follows a pattern and the more prominent (frequent) that pattern is in a language. For example, the suffix for the regular past tense in English is productive in English because most verbs form its past tense by adding it to the infinitive and because new verbs will take it. The suffix *–ar* is the most common ending for the citation (infinitive) form of verbs in Spanish, and new verbs will be *–ar* verbs in the language. An example is *alunizar* 'land on the moon', to use a term coined 51 years before this book was going to print.

Productive phenomena deserve pedagogical attention. The acquisition of a productive phenomenon is a point of reference to assess the level of proficiency of a learner. The dative is more productive in Spanish than in English. Even in English, the dative deserves explicit attention. It is a lot easier to understand dative shift (and use it as an L2 learner) the better one knows the difference between a direct object and an indirect object.

---

(8)   a.   La niña le escribió [**una carta**] a la mamá.[14]
        'The girl wrote [**a letter**] to her Mom'.
    b.   El juez le había advertido al acusado [**que no saliera de la casa**].
        'The judge had warned the accused [**not to leave his/her house**].
    c.   El juez le creyó [**la historia**] al abogado.
        'The judge believed the lawyer [**his/her story**]'.
    d.   El cazador le disparó [**un tiro**] al pato.
        'The hunter shot [**a shot**] at the duck'.
    e.   El padre les enseñó [**una lección**] a los niños.
        'The father taught the children [**a lesson**]'.

f. El asesor financiero le explicó [**los riesgos**] al cliente.
    'The financial advisor explained [**the risks**] to the customer'.

g. El niño le habló [**palabras**] al papá.[15]
    'The child spoke [**words**] to his father'.

h. Los niños le leyeron [**un cuento**] a la mamá.
    'The children read Mom [**a short story**]'.

i. El acusado le mintió al juez.[16]
    'The accused lied to the judge'.

j. El estudiante le obedeció [**las órdenes**] a la profesora.
    'The student obeyed the professor [**her orders**]'.

k. El gobierno les paga [**el sueldo**] a los empleados oficiales.
    'The government pays its employees [**their salary**]'.

l. El mediocampista le pasó [**la pelota**] al delantero.
    'The midfielder passed [**the ball**] to the forward'.

m. El jugador le pegó [**un golpe/una patada/un cabezazo**] a la pelota.
    'The player hit the ball'. (The player struck a blow to it, kicked it, headed it, etc.)

n. El sacerdote le perdonó [**los pecados**] al arrepentido parroquiano.
    'The priest forgave the repented parishioner for [**his/her sins**]'.

o. El empleado le robó [**dinero**] al banco.
    'The employee robbed the bank'.

p. El huésped les sirvió [**comida**] a los invitados.[17]
    'The host served his guests [**their food**]'.

Observe what happens when we omit the indirect object pronoun (*le/les*) in the sentences in (8), as shown in (9). Many of them sound like calques (borrowings) from English. Many native speakers will use the indirect object pronoun, and the reasons will become clear when the reader gets to the explanation that follows the examples:

(9) a. *La niña escribió a la mamá.   (The girl wrote her Mom.)

b. *El juez había advertido al acusado.   (The judge had warned the accused.)

c. *El juez creyó al abogado.   (The judge believed the lawyer.)

d. *El cazador disparó al pato.   (The hunter shot at the duck.)

e. *El padre enseñó a los niños.   (The father taught the children.)

f. *El asesor financiero explicó al cliente.   (*The financial adviser explained the customer.)

g. *El niño habló al papá.   (*The boy talked his father.)

h. *Los niños leyeron a la mamá.   (The children read to her Mom.)

i.   *El acusado mintió al juez.   (*The accused lied the judge.)

j.   %El estudiante obedeció a la profesora.   (The student obeyed the teacher.)

k.   *El gobierno paga a los empleados.   (The government paid its employees.)

l.   #El mediocampista pasó al delantero.   (The midfielder passed the forward.)

m.   *El jugador pegó la pelota.   (The player hit the ball.)

n.   %El sacerdote perdonó al arrepentido parroquiano.   (The priest forgave the repented parishioner.)

o.   *El jefe robó al empleado.   (The boss robbed the employee.)

p.   %El anfitrión sirvió a los invitados.   (The host served his guests.)

p'.   *El anfitrión sirvió los invitados.   (The host served his guests.)

Servir 'serve' shows particularly well the contribution of dative marking. If the invitees (invited) were marked with accusative (as in 10) instead of dative (as in 8p), the sentence will have accusative *a*, but it will not be duplicated with *le(s)*, and the interpretation would be clearly different:

(10) El anfitrión sirvió a los invitados.

This sentence would mean in Spanish that the host cooked the invitees and served them to someone else. It is interesting that this interpretation does not seem to come to mind in English. The robustness of dative in Spanish might be one of the factors at play. Meaning coercion might be the reason why speakers of English almost never contemplate this possibility. It is conceivable that some (perhaps many) native speakers of Spanish will produce and read sentences similar to those in (10) without realizing the interpretation of the guests as the verbed. This author conjectures that this distinction will kick in from now on for readers of this book. This distinction always kicks in for me as a teacher of language, and particularly as someone who does research on verbees.

A similar situation obtains with *pegar*. The translation for each sentence is given in the paragraph after (11), so readers who would like to try and figure out the meaning of each sentence should look at the examples but stop reading until they have seen the difference in meaning coded with the indefinite object deletion in (11a,c) as opposed to the verber/**verbed** sentences in (11b,d).

(11) a.   El jugador le pegó [una patada] al contrincante.

b.   El jugador pegó al contrincante.

    c. El jugador le pegó a la pelota.
    d. El jugador pegó la pelota.

(11b) would mean that the player glued his opponent, a highly unlikely sentence. (11d) would mean that the player glued the ball, a likely occurrence, if we have a rubber ball that can be repaired by gluing it.

    Translation for the sentences in (11) above:

(12) a. El jugador le pegó [una patada] al contrincante.
       'The player hit/struck [a kick to] his opponent'.
    b. El jugador pegó al contrincante.
       'The player glued his opponent'.
    c. El jugador le pegó a la pelota.
       'The player struck [a strike to] the ball'.
    d. El jugador pegó la pelota.
       'The player glued the ball'.

5.6. Why "<u>encantatarias</u>/encantadas" are so different from "<u>encantadores</u>/encantadas"

There are a good number of verbs in Spanish similar to English *appeal*. Those verbs have <u>verber</u>/**verbed** with one meaning and <u>verbee</u>/**verbed** with a different meaning. Thus, if we apply the test in (5a,b) above, the corresponding sentence is grammatical both with an indirect object pronoun (13a,b) and with a direct object pronoun (13d), but with a difference in meaning. An explanation of the difference in meaning is provided further below so readers can try and see the differences for themselves.

(13) a. <u>A las niñas</u> <u>les</u> encantó **el helado**.   (verbatario/verbado)
    b. **El helado** <u>les</u> encantó <u>a las niñas</u>.
    c. <u>El mago</u> encantó **a las niñas**.   (Verbador/verbado)
    d. **A las niñas las** encantó <u>el mago</u>.
    e. *<u>El mago</u> **las** encantó **a las niñas**.

Sentence (13a) means that the girls liked the ice cream a lot. Verberless *encantar* means 'like a lot' or 'fascinate'. The girls are the verbee and the ice cream the verbed. (13a) is synonymous with (13b), and the dative in (13b) is not a result of dative overriding because when the dative clitic is omitted, as in (13c), the meaning changes. Transitive *encantar* means 'cast a spell'. Now the sentence means that the magician cast a spell on the girls. He is the verber and the girls are the verbed. The transitivity of (13c) is corroborated by the grammaticality of the direct object pronoun in (13d) [*las*] and the ungrammaticality of (13e) when the pronoun duplicates a postverbal verbed. (13c) passes all of the entailments of a transitive sentence as in (1) at the beginning of this chapter. (13a) does not pass any of those entailments because it behaves like *gustar* as in (2) at the beginning of this chapter. Let us present this information as a table.

A similar contrast obtains with verberless *aprovechar* and transitive *aprovechar*, with an interesting difference in meaning stemming from the animacy alignment. Readers are invited to discover the difference. The translation for each of the sentences is provided in Table 5.6.

Interestingly, the prototypical use of the two meanings of *aprovechar* shows the animacy alignment at work: the transitive version is the typical alignment (the verber is [+H] and the **verbed** is [-H]). The intransitive one is an atypical alignment (the subject is [-H] and the object is [+H]), as Table 5.5 and Table 5.6 show. An interesting question for further research is whether these two verbs are synonymous, or their meaning is as different as that of *importar* 'import' and *importar* 'matter'. *Aprovechar*(1) and *aprovechar*(2) are similar to *appeal*(1) and *appeal*(2).

Some readers might think about sentences in Spanish like *se me apareció un fantasma* 'a ghost appeared [herself/himself] to me' and *se me ocurrió una idea* 'an idea occurred [itself] to me'. Some of those readers would want to know whether this proposal can account for them. It can. But I will leave that issue open for now. It will be a nice topic for a student to write a paper. Perhaps even an article or a thesis.

5.7. Is the only object of *ayudar* 'help' direct or indirect?

Ayudar has variable case marking in Spanish. Some speakers use a direct object pronoun with it, yet others use an indirect object with it. It appears to some speakers that *ayudar* 'help' takes verber and **verbed**, and the verbed is marked as a direct object. However, many more speakers mark the only object as if it were an indirect object.[18] There is good evidence that the one receiving some help is the benefactee, not the **verbed**. First, since the subject passes the verber test, what these speakers seem to be doing is assuming that *ayudar* is a verb with three participants whose **verbed** undergoes indefinite object deletion, as with the verbs in §5.5 above. Second, it appears that the intuition behind *ayudar* is that this verb means *dar ayuda*, and that explains why the object is expressed as an indirect object. That intuition is on the right track. RAE (2020) defines *ayudar* 'help' as *prestar cooperation* 'lend cooperation'. Third, the test discussed in §5.3 above would give conflicting results with this verb, and that is the reason why it was not included. With that test, we see this:

(14) A Isabel le/**la** ayudó <u>una actitud positiva</u>.

However, we have shown that when a [+H] object is postverbal, that object is indirect if it can (and often must) be duplicated with an indirect object pronoun, as in (15a). On the other hand, that duplication with a direct object pronoun results in ungrammaticality, as in (15b):

(15) a. <u>Una actitud positiva</u> <u>le</u> ayudó <u>a Margarita</u>.
    b. *<u>Una actitud positiva</u> **la** ayudó **a Margarita**.[19]

Remember that the only object of *helfen* 'help' and *danke* 'thank' in German is an indirect object. If *help* is *give help*, and *danke* is *give thanks*, we have accounted for the dative marking of those and similar verbs without stipulating that those verbs must be lexically marked in the LEXICON (mental vocabulary) of the language. In English, *help* is to give someone a hand. In Spanish you *give **a** hand to someone* when you help them, but you *give **the** hand to someone* when you greet them; that is, when you shake their hand.

If *ayudar* is *prestar cooperación* 'lend cooperation', then *ayudar* (like *mentir*, and the verbs in 8 above) should take an indirect object pronoun, and the sentences with <u>les</u> should sound more natural than those with **las** or **los**. Furthermore, the sentences with *les* should be more frequent. I leave that issue for further exploration to those with a focus on corpus linguistics. The sentences in (16) refer to male readers or to male and female readers. (16b) is a sentence that River Plate (Argentina and Uruguay) speakers of Spanish might say. Furthermore, (16b) should be less frequent than (16d). The sentences in (17) refer only to female speakers.

(16) a. Esta teoría les ayudará a los lectores.
    b. %Esta teoría los ayudará a los lectores.
    c. A los lectores les ayudará esta teoría.
    d. %A los lectores los ayudará esta teoría.

(17) a. Esta teoría les ayudará a las lectoras.
    b. %Esta teoría las ayudará a las lectoras.
    c. A las lectoras les ayudará esta teoría.
    d. %A las lectoras las ayudará esta teoría.

I would like to finish this chapter by thanking the reader again. With subject (nominative), direct object (accusative) and indirect object (dative), the sentence in (18e) is hard to explain. With verber, verbed, and verbee, that task is clearly easier.

(18) a.   ¡El autor <u>le</u> agradece **la atención** al lector!
'<u>The author</u> thanks <u>the reader</u> for their attention!'

    b.   ¡El autor <u>le</u> agradece <u>al lector</u>!
'<u>The author</u> thanks <u>the reader</u>!'

    c.   ¡<u>Al lector</u> <u>se</u> <u>le</u> agradece!
'<u>The reader</u>, (<u>the author</u>) thanks <u>her/him</u>!'

    d.   ¡<u>Se</u> <u>le</u> agradece <u>al lector</u>!
'<u>Someone</u> thanks <u>the reader</u>!'

    e.   ¡<u>Se</u> <u>le</u> agradece!
'<u>Someone</u> thanks <u>you</u>!'
'Thank <u>you</u>!'

5.8. Conclusions

How predictable is case marking? This proposal has shown that case marking is a lot more predictable than thought, and it has provided plenty of evidence for that claim in Spanish and English. This book has also shown some evidence for that claim in a few other languages. The explanation of case advanced in this proposal is simple, predictive, and has a great deal of motivation. Davis (2001: 2, 119) has asked one of the most revealing questions regarding case and has made a very insightful suggestion that §5.4 explores. The question is why subject and direct object cannot be reversed in countless sentences in English. The <u>verber</u> and **verbed** inferences answer that question: the participant that passes the verber inference is always the subject; the one that passes the verbed inference, the object. The suggestion (by Davis) is the observation that prepositional objects need not be part of linking or argument structure. This book has shown that prepositional objects include indirect objects, without a doubt the most controversial and studied prepositional object in linguistics. Remember that a prepositional object is an object introduced by a preposition, as in *the government counts **on** taxes, children depend **on** their parents, we belong **to** the earth, this book explained indirect objects **to** you*, etc.

It is fair to state that case marking is relatively straightforward in English; it is also fair to state that it is extremely complex in Spanish and in many other languages. The transitivity paradox is a failure to understand how case really works, as shown by countless references to "intransitive verbs" *break, freeze, melt*, and to the need for "inherent" or "lexical" indirect objects. Positing "inherent" or "lexical" indirect objects means that the learner has to memorize a few verbs that require an indirect object because those verbs do not follow a general rule. Once we have an explanation for why countless direct objects are marked as if they were indirect objects, case marking is clearer. And we already have an explanation (the verber/**verbed** inferences) for why children can use subject, direct object, and indirect object without any instruction, yet teaching and learning these notions in L2s has been a tough assignment for students, teachers, and scholars.

The difficulty in telling apart direct from indirect objects is a good hypothesis to explain, at least in part, the frustration of native speakers of English to learn an L2 in which that distinction is crucial for the grammar of that language. That distinction is very strong (i.e. explicitly needed) in languages like Arabic, Chinese, French, German, Italian, Japanese, Korean, Russian, and Spanish, to name some of the most commonly taught L2s in the world. In a sense, those languages (and probably many others) are heavy distinguishers of direct and indirect object. Native speakers of English who want to learn an L2 come from a language with an implicit understanding of subject and object (direct or indirect) in which position (subject, verb, object) codes that distinction, even in passive voice sentences. That position is reinforced by meaning: people own cars, cars do not own people; hyenas approach and eat carcasses, carcasses neither approach nor eat hyenas. Native speakers of many languages in Europe (and perhaps in most of the rest of the world) come from languages in which they can count on the help of meaning but not on position because the subject, the direct object, and the indirect object are scrambled around in many sentences.[20] That means that they know how to use clues in the sentence (other than passive voice) to determine on the fly that the preverbal participant is not necessarily the verber. Furthermore, they are used to distinguishing direct from indirect objects in their language, something that speakers of English do not have to do. In short, native speakers of English have two huge disadvantages to learn an L2 in which direct and indirect objects have to be distinguished: the lack of that distinction in their language, and the fact that subject is coded by position in English but not in many other languages. Remember also that distinguishing direct from indirect object is a lot more difficult than telling apart the subject from the direct object. That explains the competitive advantage of the rest of the world to learn an L2. In a clear way, the simplicity and beauty of English syntax, which replaced case with position, works against native speakers of English when they want to learn another language. Hopefully, the verber and verbed inferences will make this task less frustrating and more rewarding and stimulating for any L2 learner in the world. After all, verber, verbed, and verbee are constant and trackable. A more explicit understanding of the verber and verbed inferences makes learning an L2 more like learning your native language and less like learning a foreign language.

Notes

1 The sentence used in Chapter 3 was with *asustar*. Both *preocupar* and *asustar* are prototypical psych(ological) verbs. *Preocupar* is more abstract than *asustar*.

2 The absence of *les* and the presence of *a* mean that direct object marking (accusative marking) in Spanish is *a* (for a verbed that is human and definite). The presence of *les* duplicating the object means that it is an indirect object (a dative object). In terms of verber and verbed, the marker *a* means non <u>verber</u>; the presence of *les* (if mandatory) distinguishes a <u>verbee</u> from a **verbed**. This was discussed in §3.7.

3 With the present analysis, Spanish *preocupar* behaves like *temer* (that is, as a regular transitive verb) once dative overriding is factored in. The same should obtain for *preoccupare* in Italian. However, *piacere* is clearly an unaccusative verb as shown in Belletti & Rizzi (1988). That is, a verb with verbed and verbee, as the verbs in Table 4.1 (Chapter 4). The closest equivalents in English are *belong, matter, occur, seem*, etc.

4 The relative frequency of dative overriding vs. true dative is an interesting topic for research.

5 The terms *benefactee* and *malefactee* were introduced in Gil (1982). They are another term for *beneficiary* and *maleficiary*. Chapter 4 explained why *benefactee* and *malefactee* are to be preferred.

6 The first semantic roles proposed to capture the generalization over buyer, cleaner, ignorer, etc. were actor, agent, cause, effector, experiencer, instrument, force (the wind opening a door or blowing your hair), etc. Those roles were abandoned for the protoroles *Agent* and *Patient* (or the macroroles *Actor* and *Undergoer* in Role and Reference Grammar). Verber and verbed are a generalization over all of those roles, proto-roles, and macroroles, without the problems associated with them. *Cause* is not necessarily the subject, as a sentence with *fear* shows: if *students fear tests*, the cause is the object. See the conclusions to Chapter 6 on cause, verber, and subject.

7 These will be the verbs *appeal(1), appear, be, belong, cost, happen, matter, occur, remain, seem*, etc., in English.

8 *Matter* has, in turn, a transitive counterpart, *mind*.

9 I have left out verbs that tend to appear with just one participant, like *die, disappear, exist, fall, vanish*, etc. I included a few verbs of movement (*arrive, come*). If the subject is the verbed (apparently also the verber when the subject is animate), then the beneficiary or maleficiary is expected to be expressed with the dative. Thus, the mail is the arrived, but the mailperson is the arriver and the arrived. A look at verbs of movement taking dative is an issue for further research.

10 NP means noun phrase, that is, a noun and any modifiers (article, adjective, possessive pronoun) it might have.

11 Abbreviations are as follows. ACC: accusative; DAT: dative; NOM: nominative; pro: pronoun.

12 Van Hoecke (1996: 1–37) has several examples (with NOM and DAT) with the verb *be* in his discussions of the dative in Latin.

13 Remember that the NNC (Suñer 1982: 209) states that a common noun without a determiner in preverbal position cannot be the subject in Spanish (and in other languages). In other words, if the subject is preverbal and a common noun, it requires a determiner. That determiner is the definite article more often than not.

14 These verbs are not like *gustar*; they have verber, verbed, and verbee.
15 This use of *hablar* seems to come from Mexico (and perhaps neighboring countries). A Google search in May 2020 returned these results: "habló a la mamá" (78,500); "habló con la mamá" (846,000).
16 This is the only example without its verbed in brackets. *Mentir* 'tell a lie'.
17 This list is not exhaustive.
18 A simple Google search returned the following results (May 2020):
    (i)   "la ayudan" = 220,000 (7.1%)
    (ii)   "lo ayudan" = 738,000 (23.8%)
    (iii) "le ayudan" = 2,140,000 (69.01%)
19 River Plate speakers of Spanish might produce sentences similar to this one. But speakers of the rest of the Hispanic world would not produce them.
20 More than half of the world is bilingual or multilingual. Geography and grammar might be giving them a hand or two.

References

Alsina, Alex. 1996. *The role of argument structure in grammar. Evidence from Romance*. Stanford: CSLI.

Bathroom Readers' Institute. 2002. *Uncle John's biggest ever bathroom reader*. San Diego: Thunder Bay Press.

Belleti, Adriana & Rizzi, Luigi. 1988. Psych verbs and Θ-theory. *Natural Language and Linguistic Theory* 6. 291–352. (https://www.jstor.org/stable/4047649).

Comrie, Bernard. 1989. *Language universals and linguistic typology*. 2nd ed. Chicago: University of Chicago Press.

Davis, Anthony R., 2001. *Linking by types in the hierarchical lexicon*. Stanford: Center for the Study of Language and Information.

Gil, David. 1982. Case marking, phonological size, and linear order. In Hopper, Paul & Thompson, Sandra A. (eds.), *Studies in transitivity. Syntax and semantics*, vol. 15, 117–141. New York: Academic Press.

Heath, Jeffrey. 1976. Antipassivization: A functional typology. In Proceedings of the Second Annual Meeting of the Berkeley Linguistic Society, 202–211. (http://linguistics.berkeley.edu/bls/).

Jespersen, Otto. 2007[1924]. *The philosophy of grammar*. London: Routledge.

Mittwoch, Anita. 1982. On the difference between *eating* and *eating something*: Activities versus accomplishments. *Linguistic Inquiry* 13. 113–122. (https://www.jstor.org/stable/4178263).

RAE (Real Academia Española). 2020. *Diccionario de la lengua española*. Retrieved from (https://dle.rae.es) (Last accessed in 2020).

Snyder, William & Hyams, Nina. 2015. Minimality effects in children's passives. In Di Domenico, Elisa & Hamann, Cornelia & Matteini, Simona (eds.), *Structures, strategies and beyond: Essays in honour of Adriana Belletti. Vol. 223*: Linguistik Aktuell/Linguistics today, 343–368. Amsterdam: John Benjamins. https://doi.org/10.1075/la.223.

Suñer, Margarita. 1982. *Syntax and semantics of Spanish presentational sentence types*. Washington: Georgetown University Press.

Van Hoecke, Willy. 1996. The Latin dative. In Van Belle, William & Van Langendonck, Willy (eds.), *The dative. Vol. 1: Descriptive studies*, 1–37. (Case and grammatical relations across languages). Amsterdam: John Benjamins.

6 A brief comparison with some theories of linking (argument realization)

6.1. Introduction

This chapter compares briefly the present proposal with Dowty's theory of protoroles, the most invoked theory of semantic roles.[1] It also compares it with Role and Reference Grammar (RRG) and with three other proposals that proposed additions or some changes to Dowty's theory (Ackerman & Moore 1999; 2001; Beavers 2010; Primus 1999; 2012). The brevity of this comparison and the complexity of the issues at hand (how to determine macrorole, for example) will probably make this chapter slightly harder to follow than the rest of the book. As stated regarding some endnotes (and a few observations intended mostly for linguists), teachers and readers from different backgrounds need not worry if they do not see the point in a few paragraphs. The general reader or the language teacher will not be missing much, if anything at all. I trust that most of the chapter will make sense. Three first-year college students have read this chapter and have stated that they understand it to the point that they enjoyed reading it and understood some of the points made throughout the book from a new perspective.

The comparison offered here is brief, given that this proposal is advanced here for the first time, and particularly because the ECONOMY and PREDICTIVENESS of verber/verbed are uncontroversial. I anticipate that scholars will have many questions, some of which I anticipated in the book. I will try to answer as quickly as possible other questions that will surely begin to be asked as this proposal is disseminated.

> Van Valin & LaPolla (1997: 5) define economy and predictiveness regarding competing analyses in linguistics as follows:
>   ECONOMY (Occam's Razor): Is it the simplest theory?
>   PREDICTIVENESS: Do the hypotheses predict phenomena beyond those for which they were formulated?

I will retake these two criteria in the conclusions, after the reader has seen plenty of examples of the economy and predictive power of the verber and the verbed inferences vis-à-vis competing theories of how speakers determine who or what is the subject and who or what is the direct object in a sentence.

6.2. Reducing Dowty's proto-properties from ten to two simple inferences

The simpler and most invoked theory of how speakers determine who is the subject and the direct object is Dowty (1991). Some modifications to his theory have been proposed, but none of them of substance. I will briefly refer to some of those modifications later in this chapter.

According to Dowty, most linking is predictable. It follows his Argument Selection Principle (ASP), stated below, along with contributing properties for each protorole. In plain English, Dowty's theory states that in a sentence with subject and direct object, the subject is the participant with more of the properties listed in (2) and the direct object the participant with more of the properties listed in (3).[2] Dowty himself admits that some verbs are not accounted for with his ASP (See §1.2 and also Dowty's quote before example 6). The verber and the verbed inferences account for those exceptions.

(1)   Argument Selection Principle (1991: 576):

>   In predicates with grammatical subject and object, the argument for which the predicate entails the greatest number of Proto-Agent properties will be lexicalized as the subject of the predicate; the argument having the greatest number of Proto-Patient entailments will be lexicalized as the direct object.

(2)   Contributing properties for the agent protorole (572):
    a.   volitional involvement in the event or state
    b.   sentience (and/or perception)
    c.   causing an event or change of state in another participant
    d.   movement (relative to the position of another participant)
    e.   (exists independently of the event named by the verb)
(3)   Contributing properties for the patient protorole (572):
    a.   undergoes change of state
    b.   incremental theme
    c.   causally affected by another participant

d. stationary (relative to movement of another participant)
e. (does not exist independently of the event, or not at all)

Dowty's ASP accounts for most of the sentences with a [+H] subject and a [-H] direct object, which is the typical animacy alignment proposed in Chapter 3. The two sets of five properties each in (2) and (3) appear to be modeled after the Fillmore (1977: 102) series of rankings and the ten parameters of transitivity of Hopper & Thompson (1980). Those three proposals probably draw from the traditional intuition of transitivity according to which the direct object is affected or undergoes a change.[3] Although many transitive sentences express a change of state, neither change nor affectedness are necessary conditions for a sentence to be transitive. Consider (4), a sentence from Dowty (1991: 573) to exemplify causally affected:

(4) Smoking causes cancer.

Is cancer the affected? Not at all. The affected is the living organism who develops a cancer. Affectedness presupposes existence. The cancer came about due to smoking. Thus, more than affected, the cancer was caused or produced by smoking. In fact, the answer as to whether the cancer was affected or created is not in it being the object or not; it is in the verb: it was (the) caused. On the other hand, it is accurate to state that smoking affects your lungs, your health, your job, your quality of life, etc. But that is a different story: you already have your lungs, your health, your job, etc.

You are almost finished reading this book. You have read five chapters. If you think about it, who or what is more affected for having read this book? If you highlighted, underlined, and wrote some notes on this book, the book has changed. Actually, only your copy of the book was affected, not really the book. I dare say that readers change more than the books they read; even when a book is heavily highlighted, that reader has changed more than the book.

Let us suppose that you bought this book or received it as a gift. The book changed location from the store to your house. Change of location (place) has been argued to be a change; that is, the book has undergone a change of place. That is, indeed, a legitimate inference: if you bought a book (or someone gave it to you) and everything went well, that book will get to your house. However, if you have read the book, but have not done any highlighting, underlining, or have not written any notes in it, nothing relevant has happened to your copy of the book. It is conceivable that you ended up more affected than the book. Finally, let us think about some of the books that are never read. Something happened to each book if a few more copies are sold. But nothing relevant happens to each copy that is never read. And all of this assuming that this book is not an ebook, in which case the affectedness is even more remote. Who or what is more affected when you buy an ebook? You part with some money that the publisher and the author get. You and they (the publisher and the author) are more affected than the book. Paradoxically, the publisher, the author, and you are the subject of the relevant sentences. You bought an ebook, you parted with some money, the publisher and the author got that money, and you have access to a virtual copy of the book. *You* and *they*, the subject, are more affected. In fact, the affectedness is irrelevant for most purposes. As it is when that affectedness is invoked for the direct object. Affectedness was the intuition behind the specialized term in Greek (accusative) for the direct object 22 centuries ago (Butt 2006: 14). If you are reading this book, you know that the world has changed since then.

If you read books, that entails that you can read, and do read. It does not entail that books can read. You are of course the reader, and the books that you read are the read. Books do not read people. The subject and object of countless sentences cannot be reversed because animates do more things to inanimates than the other way around, and those inanimates cannot do otherwise. That answers the question posed by Davis (2001: 2) as to why the subject and object of countless sentences cannot be reversed. That is also part of the intuition captured in the [+H] verber and the [-H] **verbed** alignment, which captures the essence of the five subject proto-properties and the five direct object proto-properties without missing the right generalizations, and without making any wrong predictions, as the following discussion will show.

6.3. Psych(ological) verbs need no longer be a headache for linguists

The reader will remember sentences (2) and (3) from Chapter 3, repeated in (5) below:

(5) a. Students fear tests.
     b. Tests frighten students.

Dowty (1991: 579) goes to great lengths to try to explain *frighten*:

> What I believe sets this class of predicates off from all other natural-language verbs is that (i) the predicate entails that the Experiencer has some perception of the Stimulus—thus the Experiencer is entailed to be sentient/perceiving, though the Stimulus is not—and (ii) the Stimulus causes

some emotional reaction or cognitive judgment in the Experiencer. The first of these is a P-Agent entailment for the Experiencer, while the second is a P-Agent entailment for the Stimulus argument. Moreover, these predicates have no OTHER entailment for either argument that are relevant to argument selection (with one possible exception to be discussed directly), which leaves a situation in which each argument has a weak but apparently equal claim to subjecthood. (579; emphasis original)

EXPERIENCER: A semantic role that has been invoked, at least informally, for the subject of verbs like *fear*, the direct object of verbs like *frighten*, and the indirect object of verbs like *tell*, *show*, etc. In theory, a [+H] involved as the direct object and often as the subject of a verb of cognition, emotion, or perception (e.g. a psych verb) is an experiencer. If *you fear thunder, you* are the experiencer. If *thunder frightens you, you* are the experiencer. If *one particularly long day at work gives you a headache, you* are the experiencer. Interestingly, the role of experiencer has been attributed informally (and often formally) to subjects, direct objects, and indirect objects similar to the situations described in these three sentences about you.

Those familiar with the Universal Alignment Hypothesis (Perlmutter and Postal 1984: 97) or with the Uniformity of Theta-assignment Hypothesis (Baker 1988; 1997) will realize that invoking the experiencer role for subject, direct object, and indirect object shows that this role is not on the right track. A putative subject experiencer is a verber; and a putative direct object experiencer is a verbed. A putative indirect object experiencer need not be part of linking. Its meaning is arrived at by computing the meaning of the preposition *to* and that of the noun (and modifiers of that noun phrase).

Furthermore, when stimulus-subject verbs are INCHOATIVE (as opposed to STATIVE, an observation due to Croft (1986)), quoted by Dowty (580), Dowty continues,

[…] this inchoative interpretation entails a Proto-Patient property in the Experiencer that is not present in the stative—undergoing a (definite) change of state. Hence, though the two arguments are still equal in Agent properties, they are unequal in that one is a 'better' Patient, so it must be the direct object according to the selection principle in 31. (580)

INCHOATIVE: A verb that expresses entering a different state, as when someone blushes, becomes glad, gets angry, gets frightened, calms down, etc.

> STATIVE: A verb that expresses a state, for example, if *you own a house,*
> *love your family, like pistachio pesto pasta,* etc. No activity (no action) takes
> place with a verb of state. Verbs of state express situations that hold for a
> period of time, including one's whole life, when people love members of their
> family, for example.

As observed in the introduction to Chapter 3, native speakers do not know
that *frighten* is a Stimulus-subject verb nor do they know that *fear* is a
Stimulus-object verb. Yet native speakers and advanced L2 learners of
English use these verbs correctly, and the latter surely use the equivalent
of these two verbs in their native language, even if dative instead of accusative is involved. This is seen, for example, in Spanish for *temer* 'fear'
and *asustar* 'frighten', although both can, and are also used with accusative. Inchoativity and stativity are concepts that very few speakers know. In
short, all of the machinery necessary for explaining *fear* and *frighten* verbs
with Dowty's model is unnecessary with <u>verber</u> and **verbed**, as shown in
sentences (2) and (3) in Chapter 3.

It is interesting that Dowty (1991) does not see a need to explain *fear*.
I suppose he assumed, as apparently most linguists have, that the [+H]
subject will easily satisfy several of the subject proto-properties, and the
object will satisfy a few object proto-properties. The subject of *fear* satisfies sentience, which is a subject property. I do not think volition is satisfied
because one does not want to feel fear. However, the cause of the fear is the
object, it should be the subject. Students are the affected in an event of fear-
ing (a panic attack, for example). They are the subject, but they should be
the object. Thus, one subject property that applies is correctly aligned with
the subject, but one subject property (cause) that should apply to the subject applies to the object, and one object property (affectedness) that should
apply to the object applies to the subject.

In English, 220 verbs behave like *frighten* (Levin 1993: 38, 76, 189–
190).[4] Since *fear* verbs must have a [+H] verber but the verbed can be [-H]
or [+H], the members of the class of *fear* verbs are going to be a good few
dozen (the *admire* verbs are actually 44 in Levin 1993). The reader will
remember from sentences (2) and (3) in Chapter 3 that both verbs behave
like any regular transitive verb with the verber and verbed inferences. At
least in Spanish and English, psych verbs are better behaved than previously
believed.

With <u>verber</u> and **verbed**, it is not necessary to admit that verbs like *suffer,*
undergo, or *receive* have atypical agent subjects (a-subjects), as Manning
(1996: 36) states. Dowty (1991: 581) had already listed the following verbs
as exceptions to his ASP:

There is in fact one relatively small group of verbs, including *receive, inherit, come into (an inheritance), undergo, sustain (an injury), suffer (from), submit to, succumb to* and *tolerate*, which seem to have Goals (*receive*, etc.) or Patients (*undergo*, etc.) as subjects, but Agents or causes as other arguments. Perhaps the appropriate comment is that these are in fact exceptions; but they are few in number, so the selection principle is not an absolute rule but is nevertheless a strong tendency.

Consider these examples with "atypical" agent subjects. The corresponding passive voice is added to prove that the **verbed** is the object, although the subject is the affected. The direct object does not have to be affected because affectedness is not a necessary condition for direct objecthood.

(6) a. Uncle George suffered a heart attack.
    a'. A heart attack was suffered by Uncle George.
    b. Uncle George underwent surgery.
    b'. Surgery was undergone by Uncle George.
    c. Uncle George received superb medical attention.
    c'. Superb medical attention was received by Uncle George.

Uncle George was the sufferer, undergoer, and receiver. He was the affected, yet he is the subject. This shows clearly that affectedness is irrelevant. In this case, it is misleading. The heart attack is the suffered, the surgery is the undergone, and the superb medical attention is the received. Observe that the subject of the three sentences with *suffer, undergo,* and *receive* above passes the verber inference. So do the subject of sentences with the following verbs listed by Dowty (and others) as problems for his theory of linking (and theirs): *astonish, buy, border, comprise, contain, concern, defeat, endure, hit, inherit, kiss, lease, like, marry, overperform, receive, sell, suffer, surround, undergo, underperform, worry,* etc. The subject of any sentence with each of those verbs passes the <u>verber</u> inference. More importantly, the verber inference predicts that those verbs will have an –er noun derived from the verb.[5] Thus, astonisher, buyer, borderer, compriser, container, concerner, endurer, etc. are nouns in English. Notice that *astonish* could be a *fear* verb if the subject is animate but a *frighten* verb if inanimate (<u>*you*</u> can astonish **me** or <u>*this book*</u> can astonish **you**). Either way, the subject is the astonisher and the object is the astonished. The object must be animate, though. By the same token, the object of each of those verbs passes the **verbed** inference because each of them allows Bresnan (1982) Participle Adjective Conversion Rule (PACR). Some of those verbs are among the 23 or so listed as exceptions in Dowty (1991: 579–587). In addition, *border, concern, overperfom, underperform* (among many others) are discussed by Davis (2001). *Concern, like, worry* are a problem for the Notion Rule proposed in Wechsler (1995).[6] *Contain* and *surround* are discussed by Gruber (1976), Fillmore (1977), Jackendoff (1976; 1983; 1987; 1990), Levin & Rappaport Hovav (2005), among others. They pose problems for any theory of linking. They are not a problem for the VVASP. There is no need to stipulate that the semantic analysis of *surround* and *contain* is "derived solely from intuition", as stated by Levin & Rappaport Hovav (2005: 83) because there are not existing semantic roles that can be invoked to account for them. If a circle surrounds/contains a dot, the circle is the surrounder/container and the dot is the surrounded/contained. With the VVASP these two verbs are as well-behaved as any regular transitive verb.

Buy and *sell* have been a challenge for linking theories since semantic roles were proposed, because scholars have looked at them together. Perhaps drawing on work by Fillmore (1977: 72–74) and surely by Jackendoff (1987: 381), Dowty (556) states that the entailments for both *buyer* and *seller* "do not seem to be distinguished from each other". That is a mixing illusion, not a problem. If I sell you this idea of the <u>verber</u> and **verbed**, I am the seller, and this idea is the sold. If you buy this idea, you are the buyer, and this idea is the bought. This is the intuition at work when speakers express selling or buying events, even when the sale is an abstraction. Sellers and buyers are never confused, as a tie in proto-role properties between buyer and seller might predict. Sellers always take your money, and buyers take home goods or benefit from a service for which they pay. If buyer and seller were not clearly distinct, you could walk out of a grocery store with some groceries and more money than when you walked in. That can happen when the clerk makes a mistake in giving the buyer the correct change, but not because there is confusion as to who is the buyer and the seller.

6.4. Role and Reference Grammar (RRG) macroroles

To my knowledge, RRG is the linguistic theory that has developed in more detail and in a sizeable number of languages as a theory of linking, as in Van Valin & LaPolla (1997), and subsequent work mainly by Van Valin.[7] The fact that children know how to use subject, direct object, and indirect object before they get to Kindergarten but linguists or researchers working on syntax and semantics must be willing to invest a few dozen hours to accomplish a working knowledge of RRG's lexical semantic decomposition, as presented, for example in Foley & Van Valin (1984), Van Valin & LaPolla (1997), Van Valin (1990; 2004) argues for the VVASP's simplicity.[8] The equivalent in RRG of Dowty's proto-agent and protopatient protoroles are the macroroles ACTOR and UNDERGOER. UNDERGOER is a macrorole that captures a generalization over different types of direct objects (patient, theme, stimulus, content, desire, possessed, creation, etc.). Note that the UNDERGOER macrorole is the subject, not the direct object of the verb from which this macrorole is derived, as the reader can confirm by reviewing sentences (6a,b) above (the examples with the verb *undergo*). Finally, the VVASP does not have to stipulate variable macrorole assignment, as RRG must when the *recipient* becomes an *undergoer* in the double-object construction in English (e.g. Portero Muñoz 2003: 140; Van Valin & LaPolla 1997: 336; Van Valin 2004). The main motivation for semantic roles is that the role remains constant regardless of whether a participant is expressed as the subject, the direct object, or the indirect object, as the Sandra Bullock sentences show. A recipient (benefactee) in English cannot become an undergoer (verbed) because the indirect object is a benefactee who cannot become an undergoer (a **verbed**) with dative shift because the role is constant, regardless of the grammatical relation used to express it, when an option is available. The VVASP obviates the need for such a stipulation in macrorole assignment.

"ACTOR and UNDERGOER are generalized semantic roles whose prototypes are the thematic relations AGENT and PATIENT, respectively". "The single argument of an intransitive can be either actor or undergoer" (Van Valin & LaPolla 1997: 143).

ACTOR and UNDERGOER correspond to verber and verbed with two differences. Verber and verbed are derived as entailments (logical inferences) from any sentence. Determining ACTOR and UNDERGOER involves determining Aktionsart, lexical decomposition, logical form, etc. I have indicated above two problems with UNDERGOER. Only linguists understand ACTOR and UNDERGOER. It is completely unrealistic to use these terms to teach a second language. The fact that children understand and produce passive voice sentences without any instruction supports the claim that they are applying the verbed inference.

6.5. Primus protorecipient

Primus (1999) was on the right track in addressing the need for a semantic protorole for dative-marked objects. It is not a surprise that such a proposal came from a linguist specializing in German, a language with robust dative marking. She proposed a third protorole called a PROTORECIPIENT, which captures the generalization of *addressee, goal,* and *benefactee* but misses *source* and *malefactee*. She also sees the need to invoke a role of *experiencer* in her "meaning postulates" to spell out the linking of verbs like *tell* or *show*, in which possession is not transferred (1999: 54–55). Her meaning postulates for *Peter gave Mary an apple* and *Peter told Mary the secret* are as in (7) below. This notation should not intimidate the reader, as the explanation that follows shows:

(7)   a. $\forall x \forall y \forall z$[GIVE(x, y, z) → P-CONTROL(x, BECOME(POSS (y, z)))]
      b. $\forall x \forall y \forall z$[TELL(x, y, z) → P-CONTROL(x, BECOME(EXPER (y, z)))]

This notation means, roughly, that for all x, for all y, and for all z, a participant "x intends to bring about that y hears z" (Primus 1999: 55).[9] Her claim that "possession is not transferred" in sentences with *tell* and *show* is questionable. If someone tells you a secret, a joke, (or gives you) a piece of information, you have been given that secret, joke, or piece of information, and you own them. Invoking EXPER(iencing) as part of the explanation for telling **something** to someone seems an unnecessary stipulation. Thus, (7b) can be covered with the formula in (7a). There is a transfer of an abstraction when someone tells you a secret, a joke, or shows you a book, a passage in a book, or how to do something.

Although the proposal of a protorecipient made sense a few years ago, this proposal has shown that such a role is not needed, at least as part of a theory of linking. We showed that the task of the speaker is determining who the subject is and who the direct object is. The indirect object is marked (i.e. introduced, mediated) by a preposition, which can be omitted, but indirect objecthood is still visible in a pronoun "duplicating" that indirect object in languages like Spanish. The computation of the meaning of the preposition plus its object is done by putting together the meaning of each part. In English, people bake cakes for other people but not *to other people. The intuition of benefactee (or malefactee) is so strong that even when someone says that *she baked Lila a cake*, it does not occur to any listener or reader that Lila went into an oven. Suppose *we send a book to Boston[i] for her newborn*, Boston[i] being Mara Boston, a former student of mine. If we had to do linking for indirect objects, we might have to answer the question as to whether *for her newborn* could potentially count as a second indirect object in that sentence, an observation that nobody has mentioned, to the best of my knowledge. If linking needs to distinguish only subject from direct object, we do not have to answer that question. We simply compute the meaning of *to Boston[i]* and *for her newborn* COMPOSITIONALLY, the word that linguists use to assign meaning to a string of words (in the right order) by putting together the meaning of each of them, which is what we as speakers do all the time. Except, crucially, for subject and direct object, in which directionality (coded by position) contributes to the meaning. If I say that *my wife looks like Anne Hathaway*, a few people might take me seriously. However, if I were to say that *Anne Hathaway looks like my wife*, people will know that I am kidding or an idiot. These two sentences show how important position is in English to code differences in meaning. In short, as §4.5 showed, indirect objects need not be part of linking, the question of who the subject is and who the direct object is in a sentence.

6.6. Beavers (2010) proposal to change Dowty's protopatient properties

Beavers (2010) proposes to change Dowty's proto-patient properties (the ones in 3 above) for the four properties in (8), each exemplified in (9). The examples in (9) come from Beavers (2010), as indicated:

(8) a. Undergoes QUANTIZED change[10]
     b. Undergoes NONQUANTIZED change[11]
     c. Has POTENTIAL for change
     d. Is TOTALLY TRAVERSED
(9) a. The tailor lengthened the jeans to 32ins. (ex. 29, p. 834)
     b. The tailor lengthened the jeans. (ex. 30, p. 834)
     c. John hit/slapped the car, but nothing changed about the car. (ex. 35b, p. 834)
     d. John climbed the stairs. (ex. 84, p. 852)

Observe that the quantizing is contributed by "to 32ins". The tailor will always be the subject and lengthener, and the jeans the lengthened. In the absence of any mention of the effect of the hitting or slapping of the car, listeners/readers will infer that no relevant damage occurred. If damage occurred, it would be explicitly mentioned; however, the direct object can be the same. Beavers writes that when *John climbs the stairs*, the stairs are not affected. On the other hand, he adds, John is "affected" because he has changed location. John's change of location is an IMPLICATURE if he climbed the stairs. Invoking affectedness for John in (9d) is not only irrelevant; it also adds to the evidence that affectedness (or change) is neither an exclusive property of the direct object nor is it a necessary property of it, as shown by (9c,d) and (10b) below, and by several other sentences discussed in this book. For example, nothing has happened to Anne Hathaway when this author has said several times in class during the last few years that my wife looks like her. Anne Hathaway does not know who on earth this writer is.

> IMPLICATURE: An implicature is anything that is inferred from an UTTERANCE but that is not a condition for the truth of the utterance.
> UTTERANCE: An utterance is a natural unit of speech bounded by breaths or pauses.
> (Both of these definitions come from SIL 2020).

Therefore, the implicatures of *John climbed the stairs* are that he changed location, and that he is upstairs, if we have not indicated that he came back down.

Beavers (2010: 852) proceeds to explain that traversal can also be (a) totally traversed, (b) traversed, (c) potentially traversed, or (d) unspecified (for traversal). Readers can probably infer by now that these changes to Dowty's proto-patient properties are unnecessary. All of these objects are the verbed, and whether they are affected is the contribution of the meaning of the verb, not the result of whether the sentence has a direct object or not. Consider these three simple sentences:

(10) a.   John dented the car.
    b.   John admired the car.
    c.   The windshield cracked.

The car is affected in (10a) but not in (10b), yet subject and direct object are the same in both sentences. The windshield is affected in (10c). When one notices a crack on a windshield, there is a good chance that one does not know the cause. Most of the times, it is probably irrelevant. The windshield is the cracked, and it is affected but more because of the meaning of the verb than because it is an object (that can be expressed as a subject, as in 10c). It is not easy to imagine a windshield cracking anything in the normal use of a windshield attached to a car. Consider the sentences in (11), which seem to show the motivation for an unaccusativization without the form of the passive voice (was cracked):

(11) a.   The windshield was cracked. (= the windshield got cracked). (Passive voice)
    b.   The windshield was cracked.
       (Resultative sentence. We bought a used car, and the windshield had already a crack. The intended meaning is that the windshield has a crack).
    c.   The windshield cracked.
       (One day, we noticed a crack that we had not seen, and we told our spouse about it).

In summary, the modifications proposed by Beavers might be an improvement to Dowty's proposal but fall short of being as simple by sheer number as the verbed inference in order to determine who is the direct object in a sentence. Furthermore, the difference in Quantized and Nonquantized change in (9a,b) is not in the direct object, but in the ADJUNCT "by 32ins".

ADJUNCT: "An adjunct, broadly defined, is an optional constituent of a construction" (SIL 2020). Williams (2015: 194) states that, "By definition, an adjunct cannot be specified in the lexical properties of a verb". RAE (2020) defines a circumstantial complement as, "Each of the syntactic functions performed by the phrases not selected semantically by the verb to which they modify, such as place, time, or manner". (Translation by the author.) A phrase, omissible in principle, which adds a *CIRCUMSTANTIAL* detail to a sentence. *Circumstantial* is the term used commonly in traditional Spanish grammar for adjuncts, which are called *circumstantial complements. Complement* is, in turn, the most common word in Spanish grammar for *object*. The *direct object* is called in Spanish grammar the *complemento directo*.

6.7. Ackerman & Moore's Bounding Entity

This comparison is brief, but I knew that a comparison would be expected. Due to its brevity, it is impossible to do justice to the proposals just reviewed (Beavers, Dowty, Primus, RRG) with a page or a couple of paragraphs. It is particularly unfair to do that with Ackerman & Moore because their proposal puts together insights from Dowty and from Lexical Functional Grammar (LFG). Therefore, instead of butchering Lexical Mapping Theory (LMT) from LFG in a couple of pages, I would like to mention to those who would like to see a comparison with Ackerman & Moore's work that I have already written a draft of an answer to their work on causative constructions, at least for Spanish. But I need to review the research on causatives before I can send that answer out to publication. That might have to wait for a sabbatical leave in 2022 or 2023. Perhaps some five years from now (2020).

Two brief observations can be quickly made. Ackerman & Moore (1999; 2001) propose to add Bounding Entity as an object property to Dowty's proto-patient properties in (3). Only a reduction in Dowty's proto-properties to one property for subject and one property for direct object will be a proposal that can be compared with the verber and verbed inferences. Furthermore, on the issue of weighting proto-properties, consider these sentences:

(12) a.   Cecilia opened the door.
    b.   The key opened the door.
    c.   The wind opened the door.
    d.   The remote control opened the door.
    e.   The door opened.

A subject can be more or less proto-agentive (i.e. a prototypical subject), as (12a-d) show, but it is a subject or it is not. The instrument in (12b) is manipulated and comes into direct contact with the door, but a remote control is never in physical contact with a door it opens. In a sense, the wind comes into contact with a regular door when it is strong enough to push it open. However, it is hard to imagine the wind opening a garage door opened by a remote control. There is no gradualness to a subject, regardless of whether that subject is prototypical or not. It is either in the sentence or not. As (12e) clearly shows, the "agent" does not even have to be there. However, (12e) has a subject, but that subject is of course a verbed. In other words, a subject can be more or less agentive, as (12a-d) show, but it is a subject when it is in the sentence (even if simply implied, as in pro-drop languages) or it is not. The same way that affectedness is not a necessary condition for objecthood, agentiveness is not a necessary condition for subjecthood. The subject of (12e) is the underlying object of most sentences with *open* and *door*. If we wanted to express that observation in terms of verber and verbed, we simply say that the subject of (12e) is the verbed.

6.8.   Some implications for linguistic theory and for language teaching

Two implications are particularly important. First, the implication that the task of linguistic theory is now determining how speakers know their verber and verbed is simpler than the current task of accounting for subject, direct object, and indirect object. Remember that in English the indirect object is marked with a preposition. When the preposition can be left out, it is uncontroversial who/what is the verbed (the secondary object = the direct object) and who is the beneficiary or maleficiary (the primary object = indirect object). Having to distinguish just subject from direct object is a simplification of one third in sheer number. If one thinks about the complexity of distinguishing direct object from indirect object using our current understanding of linguistics, that simplification is even greater. This implication is particularly relevant for linguistic theory.

    Second, Davis (2001: 87) estimates that if speakers were using Dowty's (1991) five subject proto-properties and five direct object proto-properties to determine subject and direct object, speakers would be computing 2,592 possible dyadic combinations of subject and direct object. And this does not take into account the indirect object. The verber and the **verbed** inferences divide that number by two, which means that the present proposal is a simplification, at least in theory, of 1,296 times. In practice, that simplification is hard to quantify, but it makes a provocative issue for research. For example, with a rule of verber reflexivization (Whitley & González 2016), the ten to fifteen different types of reflexive sentences in Spanish are reduced to one. That is a simplification in sheer number of at least ten. Those familiar with the different functions of SE in Spanish (SE being a cover term for any form of the reflexive pronoun in the language) should agree that ten can be multiplied at least by ten if we would like to factor in the simplification in terms of understanding the underlying phenomena. The simplification of going from computing 2,592 possible dyadic combinations of subject and direct object to applying two simple inferences is particularly relevant for L2 learning.

Finally, the test of the tools is the following. Is the L2 learner working with verber and **verbed** or with subject, direct object, and indirect object? Is second language learning (or acquisition) as easy and as remarkable as native language acquisition? Clearly not. The latter is natural, easy, effortless, and remarkably efficient. L2 learning is a lot of work. The verber and the **verbed** inferences are not going to make learning an L2 quite as easy as one's native language, but the difference will be significant. With verber and **verbed**, it will be so much easier to stay on task. Staying on task until that task is enjoyable – or because it is rewarding and enjoyable – is a common denominator of the best L2 learners I have observed in my almost forty years of teaching and, above all, in my sixty some years of learning.

6.9. Conclusions

In a way, this book is about stating the Unaccusative Hypothesis (UH) in terms of meaning (the only participant of many intransitive sentences is the verbed) rather than in terms of form (the subject of many intransitive sentences is the underlying direct object).[12] By stating the UH in terms of verber and verbed, we make it understandable to just about anyone who can read. A good understanding of the UH is the heart of *The Fundamentally Simple Logic of Language*.[13]

Economy and predictiveness are two (out of three) of the evaluation criteria discussed by Van Valin & LaPolla (1997: 5) to compare competing linguistic analyses. In terms of economy, the verber and the verbed inferences are clearly simpler than computing Dowty's ten proto-properties. In terms of predictiveness, the two inferences also fare better than any proposal that this author is aware of.

Let us end with the notion of causation, which is perhaps the proto-property with the most predictive power (in Dowty 1991, and in others who have discussed it). It is true that regardless of volitionality (which in turn implies animacy), the cause is overwhelmingly the subject, as many scholars have observed (Davis & Koenig 2000; Levin & Rappaport Hovav 1988; Croft 1991; among others). Dowty (1991: 572) has "causing an event or change of state in another participant" as a protoagent property (a subject property) and "causally affected by another participant" as a protopatient property (a direct object property). However, sentences as common as the following show that the cause is the direct object, not the subject.

(13) a.   Students fear tests.
      b.   Many people admire Greta Thunberg.
      c.   Andrés enjoys the smell of barbecue.
      d.   Sara likes pistachio pesto pasta.

Without a doubt, causation is the proto-property with the highest predictive power of Dowty's (1991) ten proto-properties. However, it makes the wrong prediction regarding sentences like those in (13a-d). The verber and the verbed inferences predict the correct assignment of subject and direct object when verbs and nouns are put together: the verber is always the subject of the sentence, but it is not always the cause, as (13a-d) and surely countless other sentences show. Relatively very few people will probably know whom Greta Thunberg admires. On the other hand, most of those who know Greta Thunberg will easily agree with a statement similar to (13b). If asked who the cause of the admiration is, the answer is completely predictable. Simple world knowledge. *Fundamentally simple logic.* If we ask a six-year old child, who has never heard the words *sentence, subject, direct object, verber,* and *verbed* the question, "who is the subject and who is the direct object in (13a-d)?", that child might be at a loss to answer our question. If we ask that child who is the fearer and the feared, the admirer and the admired, the smeller and the smelled, and the liker and the liked, the child will have a better shot of completing the task. That child will simply have to apply the verber and the verbed inferences, something that children (and all of us) do all the time because those two inferences are the heart of *The Fundamentally Simple Logic of Language.*

Notes

1 A search on Google Scholar in 2015 showed citations as follows: Dowty (1991) = 3,647; Van Valin (1990) = 663. Several comparable articles have fewer than

200 citations. The two following books are on linking: Davis (2001) = 221, Wechsler (1995) = 221/274. Macroroles were proposed in a book by Foley & Van Valin (1984) = 2,012. Thus, citations about macroroles are surely a fraction of that book. Jackendoff's *Semantics and cognition* (1983) = 4,587. Citations about thematic roles are also probably a fraction of the citations for this book as well.

2 In later work, Dowty proposed that the properties should be weighted. Other scholars (Ackerman & Moore 1999; 2001; among others) invoked formally or informally that weighting should be incorporated. With the present proposal, the weighting is unnecessary.

3 Butt (2006: 14) reminds us that the original meaning in Greek of the accusative (the direct object) was the "affected". "Undergoing a change" might be a coinage from the last half of the 20th century.

4 The same list of 220 verbs appears three times.

5 The idea for the verber inference came from the observation by several scholars (Farrell 1994; Ryder 1999, among others) that every verb whose subject is truly agentive (ergative verbs) allows –er noun formation. I turned that observation into the verber inference.

6 In principle, all verbs with a [-H] verber and a [+H] verbed will not be accounted for by the Notion Rule. Roughly, the Notion Rule states that the subject has a notion of the direct object, but not the other way around.

7 Most of *Syntax: Structure, meaning and function* (Van Valin & LaPolla, 1997) is on linking, some of it directly and some of it indirectly. That book has 741 pages (713 + i-xxviii).

8 The claim here is that lexical semantic decomposition is not necessary to determine subject and direct object, not that it is not needed in linguistic theory.

9 Primus gives the example with *show* (*x brings about that y sees z*). I believe *tell* is clearer to show the point of transfer. However, it is also clear that if you show me something, you give me an image (or an object that I can see).

10 Beavers (2011) states that *quantized* and *nonquantized* come from Hay et al. (1999). *Traversed* is discussed in Dowty (1991).

11 The intuition behind quantized change seems to be quantifiable change. As the examples show, these sentences can be accounted for with the difference between accomplishment/achievement and activity. Affectedness is a contribution of the meaning of the verb, not of the presence of a direct object. A pizza that is dropped is affected; a pizza that is contemplated is not.

12 If *intransitivized* is used instead of *intransitive*, the statement can simply read, "the subject of ALL intransitivized sentences is the verbed". That will include unaccusative verbs (*appear, belong, cost,* etc.), passive voice (*this chapter was reviewed many times*), middle voice (*this book reads effortlessly*), etc. It would not include sentences like *Sandra Bullock was given an Oscar*. A little fix will solve that problem, "the subject of ALL intransitivized sentences is not the verber". It makes good sense to state that unaccusative sentences are intransitivized, but that ergative sentences are intransitive.

13 Remember that the Unaccusative Hypothesis is the discovery that the subject of many sentences is the verbed. The verb is verberless (*arrive, appear, belong,* etc.) or the verber was left out (*this book was published in 2021; this book will end soon*).

References

Ackerman, Farrell & Moore, John. 1999. Syntagmatic and paradigmatic dimensions of causee encodings. *Linguistics and Philosophy* 22. 1–44. (https://www.jstor.org/stable/25001731).

Ackerman, Farrell & Moore, John. 2001. *Proto-properties and grammatical encoding: A correspondence theory of argument selection*. Stanford: Center for the Study of Language and Information.

Baker, Mark. 1988. *Incorporation: A theory of grammatical function changing*. Chicago: University of Chicago Press.

Baker, Mark. 1997. Thematic roles and syntactic structure. In Haegeman, Liliane (ed.), *Elements of grammar. Handbook of generative syntax*, 73–137. Dordrecht: Kluwer Academic. https://doi.org/10.1007/978-94-011-5420-8_2.

Beavers, John. 2010. The structure of lexical meaning: Why semantics really matters. *Language* 86. 821–864. (https://www.jstor.org/stable/40961719).

Beavers, John. 2011. On affectedness. *Natural Language and Linguistic Theory* 29. 335–370. (https://www.jstor.org/stable/41475291).

Bresnan, Joan. 1982. The passive in lexical theory. In Bresnan, Joan (ed.), *The mental representation of grammatical relations*, 3–86. Cambridge, MA: MIT Press.

Butt, Miriam. 2006. *Theories of case*. New York: Cambridge University Press.

Croft, William. 1986. Surface subject choice of mental verbs. Paper presented at the Annual Meeting of the Linguistics Society of America, New York.

Croft, William. 1991. *Syntactic categories and grammatical relations. The cognitive organization of information*. Chicago: University of Chicago Press.

Davis, Anthony R. 2001. *Linking by types in the hierarchical lexicon*. Stanford: Center for the Study of Language and Information.

Davis, Anthony R. & Koenig, Jean-Pierre. 2000. Linking as constraints on word classes in a hierarchical lexicon. *Language* 76. 56–91. https://www.jstor.org/stable/417393

Dowty, David. 1991. Thematic proto-roles and argument selection. *Language* 67. 547–619. (https://www.jstor.org/stable/pdf/415037).

Farrell, Patrick. 1994. *Grammatical relations and thematic roles*. New York: Garland.

Fillmore, Charles J. 1977. The case for case reopened. In Cole, Peter & Sadock, Jerald (eds.), *Syntax and semantics: Grammatical relations*, vol. 8, 59–91. New York: Academic Press. (http://www.icsi.berkeley.edu/pubs/ai/casefor277.pdf).

Foley, William A. & Van Valin, Robert D., Jr. 1984. *Functional syntax and universal grammar*. Cambridge: Cambridge University Press.

Gruber, Jeffrey S. 1976. *Lexical structures in syntax and semantics*. Amsterdam: North-Holland.

Hay, Jennifer & Kennedy, Christopher & Levin, Beth. 1999. Scalar structure underlies telicity in "degree achievements". In Matthews, Tanya & Strolovich, Devon (eds.), The Proceedings of SALT IX, 127–144. Ithaca: Cornell University. https://doi.org/10.3765/salt.v9i0.2833.

Hopper, Paul J. & Thompson, Sandra A. 1980. Transitivity in grammar and discourse. *Language* 56. 251–295. (https://www.jstor.org/stable/413757).

Jackendoff, Ray. 1976. Toward an explanatory semantic representation. *Linguistic Inquiry* 1. 89–150. (https://www.jstor.org/stable/pdf/4177913.pdf)

Jackendoff, Ray. 1983. *Semantics and cognition*. Cambridge, MA: MIT Press.

Jackendoff, Ray. 1987. The status of thematic relations in linguistic theory. *Linguistic Inquiry* 18. 369–411. (https://www.jstor.org/stable/4178548).

Jackendoff, Ray. 1990. *Semantic structures*. Cambridge, MA: MIT Press.

Levin, Beth. 1993. *English verb classes and alternations*. Chicago: The University of Chicago Press. See also (http://www-personal.umich.edu/~jlawler/levin.html). (A verb index to use with this book).

Levin, Beth & Rappaport, Malka. 1988. Non-event –er nominals: A probe into argument structure. *Linguistics* 26. 1067–1083. (https://doi.org/10.1515/ling.1988.26.6.1067).

Levin, Beth & Rappaport Hovav, Malka. 2005. *Argument realization*. Cambridge: Cambridge University Press.

Manning, Christopher. 1996. *Ergativity, argument structure, and grammatical relations*. Stanford: Center for the Study of Language and Information.

Perlmutter, David M. & Postal, Paul M. 1984. The 1-advancement exclusiveness law. In Perlmutter, David M. & Rosen, Carol G. (eds.), *Studies in Relational Grammar*, vol. 2, 81–125. Chicago: University of Chicago Press.

Portero Muñoz, Carmen. 2003. Derived nominalizations in –ee: A role and reference grammar based semantic analysis. *English Language and Linguistics* 7. 129–159. https://doi.org/10.1017/S1360674303211059.

Primus, Beatrice. 1999. *Cases and thematic roles. Ergative, accusative and active*. Berlin: de Gruyter. https://doi.org/10.1515/9783110912463.

Primus, Beatrice. 2012. Animacy, generalized semantic roles, and differential object marking. In Lamers, Monique & de Swart, Peter (eds.), *Case, word order, and prominence. Interacting cues in language production and comprehension*, 65–90. Dordrecht: Springer. https://doi.org/10.1007/978-94-007-1463-2_4.

RAE (Real Academia Española). 2020. *Diccionario de la lengua española*. Retrieved from (https://dle.rae.es) (Last accessed 2020).

Ryder, Mary Ellen. 1999. Bankers and blue-chippers: an account of –er noun formations in present-day English. *English Language and Linguistics* 3(2). 269–297. https://doi.org/10.1017/S1360674399000246.

SIL (Summer Institute of Linguistics). 2020. Summer Institute of Linguistics. *Glossary*. Retrieved from https://glossary.sil.org/term/implicature (Last accessed 2020).

Van Valin, Robert D., Jr. 1990. Semantic parameters of split intransitivity. *Language* 66. 221–260. (https://www.jstor.org/stable/414886).

Van Valin, Robert D., Jr. 2004. Semantic macroroles in role and reference grammar. In Van Valin, Robert D., Jr. & Lapolla, Randy J. 1997. *Syntax: Structure, meaning and function*. Cambridge: Cambridge University Press.

Van Valin, Robert D., Jr. & LaPolla, Randy J. 1997. *Syntax: Structure, meaning and function*. Cambridge: Cambridge University Press.

Wechsler, Stephen. 1995. *The semantic basis of argument structure*. Stanford: Center for the Study of Language and Information.

Whitley, M. Stanley & González, Luis. 2016. *Gramática para la composición*. 3rd ed. Washington, DC: Georgetown UP.

Williams, Alexander. 2015. *Arguments in syntax and semantics*. Cambridge: Cambridge University Press. (Key topics in syntax). https://doi.org/10.1017/CBO9781139042864.

Glossary

ACCUSATIVE CASE: the case of the participant that passes the **verbed** inference. Per Burzio's Generalization (Burzio 1986: 178), "All and only the verbs that can assign a θ-role to the subject can assign accusative Case to an object". In plain English, a sentence can have a direct object only if it also has a subject. In Spanish, an animate direct object is marked with the accusative case when it is definite: (*nosotros*) *vimos a la niña* 'we saw the girl'; *vimos a Isabel* 'we saw Isabel'. The '**a**' preceding *la niña* and *Isabel* means that *la niña* and *Isabel* are the seen (the accusative). Gente 'people' in *vimos gente en la calle* 'we saw people in the street' does not have accusative case because it is indefinite.

ACTOR: a semantic role invoked as a prototypical role for the subject. In Role and Reference Grammar, "ACTOR and UNDERGOER are generalized semantic roles whose prototypes are the thematic relations AGENT and PATIENT, respectively". "The single argument of an intransitive can be either actor or undergoer" (Van Valin & LaPolla 1997: 143).

ADJUNCT: "An adjunct, broadly defined, is an optional constituent of a construction" (SIL 2020). Williams (2015: 194) states that, "By definition, an adjunct cannot be specified in the lexical properties of a verb". RAE (2020) defines a circumstantial complement as, "Each of the syntactic functions performed by the phrases not selected semantically by the verb to which they modify, such as place, time, or manner". (Translation by the author.) Adjuncts do not have semantic role (they are never a macrorole or a protorole).

AGENT: a semantic role invoked as a prototypical role for the subject. The agent protorole in Dowty (1991) corresponds, loosely speaking, to the actor macrorole of Role and Reference Grammar (Foley & Van Valin 1984; Van Valin & LaPolla 1997). See Chapter 6 for a brief discussion of Dowty's protoroles, and Role and Reference Grammar's macroroles.

ANIMACY ALIGNMENT: an alignment of <u>verber</u> and **verbed**, and animacy. See §3.1.

ARGUMENT REALIZATION (ARGUMENT STRUCTURE; LINKING): the part of linguistics that deals with the problem of who is the subject, the direct object, and the indirect object in a sentence. With this proposal, indirect object need not be part of argument realization. See §4.5.

BENEFICIARY (BENEFACTEE): the semantic role of the indirect object. The beneficiary receives something or loses it. When the latter, it is called a maleficiary. This role is not needed with the present proposal. A putative role of VERBEE captures the generalization over a beneficiary/benefactee role and a maleficiary/malefactee role, in turn a generalization over recipient, goal, experiencer, possessor, source, etc. See §4.5.

CASE: the subject (*They* in *They sent **a book** <u>to Mara Boston</u>*) is marked with the NOMINATIVE case. The direct object (**a book**) is marked with the ACCUSATIVE case. The indirect object (<u>to Mara Boston</u>) is marked with the DATIVE case. See also DATIVE SHIFT below. The accusative case is seen in English only when the direct object is a pronoun. *Her* is marked with the accusative in *he saw her* (*He saw she).

COMPOSITIONALITY (PRINCIPLE OF): the meaning of an expression is determined by its structure and the meaning of its parts. See https://plato.stanford.edu/entries/compositionality/#FregContPrin for a recently updated explanation of Frege's Principle of Compositionality. Idioms are not compositional.

DATIVE CASE: *see* CASE.

DATIVE OVERRIDING OF THE ACCUSATIVE: the use of an indirect object pronoun (*le*) instead of a direct object pronoun (*lo*) when the latter is a masculine singular referent. This is dialectal *leísmo*. When the <u>verber</u> is inanimate, this phenomenon is not restricted to the use of *le* instead of *lo*. *Le* or *les* can be used instead of *la*, *las*, *los*, *las*. This is general *leísmo*. See §3.3–3.4.

DATIVE SHIFT: the permutation of the <u>indirect object</u> (which also loses its <u>to</u> or <u>for</u>) with the **direct object**. *They sent* <u>Mara Boston</u> **a book** is the dative-shift version of <u>They</u> sent **a book** <u>to Mara Boston</u>.

DIALECTAL LEÍSMO: *see* DATIVE OVERRIDING OF THE ACCUSATIVE.

DIRECT OBJECT: the participant marked with the accusative case (***her*** in *They saw **her***). In Greek, the direct object was the *affected* participant, which was translated into Latin as the *accused*; hence the term *accusative*.

DITRANSITIVE SENTENCE: a sentence with a <u>VERBER</u>, a **VERBED**, and a <u>VERBEE</u> is ditransitive. <u>The author</u> sent <u>Mara Boston</u> **this book**. (= <u>The author</u> sent **this book** <u>to Mara Boston</u>). The second syntactic alternation is called the prepositional object alternation of a double object sentence.

DOUBLE OBJECT CONSTRUCTION: see dative shift. Dryer (1986) called the two objects in a double object construction the PRIMARY OBJECT (<u>Mara Boston</u>) and the SECONDARY OBJECT (**this book**).

ENTAILMENT: A more specialized term for INFERENCE. A sentence X entails a sentence Y if every time X is true, Y is also true (Huddleston & Pullum 2002: 35). *You bought this book* entails *this book was bought by you*.

ERGATIVE: in ergative languages (a relatively small number of languages in the world, and English is not one of them), the <u>VERBER</u> of transitive sentences is marked with the ergative case (a short suffix). When the **VERBED** is omitted, the ergative suffix is omitted; that is, the <u>VERBER</u> unergativizes.

EXPERIENCER: the [+H] who experiences an emotion (as subject, as with *fear*, or as direct object, as with *frighten*). A role of EXPERIENCER is also invoked for the referent of the indirect object of many sentences. A role of experiencer is not needed with the <u>verber</u> and **verbed** inferences, as Chapters 3-6 show.

GENERAL LEÍSMO: *see* DATIVE OVERRIDING OF THE ACCUSATIVE.

GOAL: one of the semantic roles proposed for the indirect object. Recipient and beneficiary are also roles proposed for the indirect object. The <u>VERBEE</u> role proposed in this book captures the generalization over goal, recipient, beneficiary, maleficiary, experiencer, possessor, source, etc. If *tú me robas el reloj a mí* ('if you steal the watch from me' [literally, 'if you steal the watch to me' = if you steal my watch]), I am the source. In languages in which taking away is expressed as an indirect object, the maleficiary will be the source (the person from whom something is taken away).

GRAMMATICAL RELATIONS: subject, direct object, and indirect object are the three grammatical relations recognized in virtually all linguistic theories.

INCHOATIVE: a verb that expresses entering a different state, as when someone blushes, becomes glad, gets angry, gets frightened, calms down, etc.

INFERENCE: a sentence B is an inference from a sentence A if every time A is true, B is also true. If *you bought this book*, then it is also true that *this book was bought by you*. See ENTAILMENT.

INTRANSITIVIZED: a transitive sentence, one of whose two participants has been omitted. *The door (was) opened* is an intransitivization of *Lila opened the door*.

INTRANSITIVE: a sentence that typically has just a verber (the typical sentence with verbs like *cough, sneeze, yawn, run*, etc.) or just a verbed (*die, fall, belong, happen*, etc.).

LINKING: *see* ARGUMENT REALIZATION.

MACROROLES: *see* ACTOR and UNDERGOER. It is worth noting that macroroles were proposed by Foley & Van Valin (1984) and protoroles were proposed by Dowty (1991).

NOMINATIVE CASE: the subject is said to be marked with the nominative case. The verber is always marked with the nominative case (in accusative languages). See ERGATIVE.

PATIENT: Dowty's proto-agent and protopatient protoroles correspond closely to the macroroles ACTOR and UNDERGOER. UNDERGOER is a macrorole that captures a generalization over different types of direct objects (patient, theme, stimulus, content, desire, possessed, creation, etc.). However, an UNDERGOER and a PROTOPATIENT are determined by different procedures. See Chapter 6.

PROTOROLES: see §6.1–6.3 for a brief discussion of protoroles. The discrete semantic roles of actor or agent (actor, agent, cause, instrument, force, stimulus, etc.) were replaced by protoroles. Likewise for the semantic roles of patient or theme (patient, theme, stimulus, content, desire, possessed, creation, etc.). See also MACROROLES, ACTOR, UNDERGOER.

PSYCHOLOGICAL (PSYCH) VERBS: verbs that express cognition, emotion, or perception. *Fear* and *frighten* are the two prototypical psych verbs. If the **verbed** of *astonish* is animate, *astonish* would be a *frighten* verb; if both verber and **verbed** are animate, *astonish* would be a *fear* verb.

QUANTIZE: quantify. A quantized change means a change that is quantifiable, as when a tailor lengthens a pair of jeans to 32ins. (Beavers 2010: 834.)

RECIPIENT: one of about seven semantic roles proposed for the indirect object. A role of <u>VERBEE</u> captures the generalization over the seven or so roles proposed for the indirect object (goal, experiencer, beneficiary, maleficiary, possessor, recipient, source).

REFERENT: the person, concept, or thing that a word denotes. The word *chair* denotes an object on which we sit to work, eat, rest, talk, etc.

STATIVE: A verb that expresses a state, for example, if *you own a house, love your family, like pistachio pesto pasta*, etc. No activity (no action) takes place with a verb of state.

TOPICALIZATION: the expression of the **verbed** or the <u>verbee</u> before the verb, the position called TOPIC in a sentence. *<u>Sandra Bullock</u> was given an Oscar* is <u>verbee</u> topicalization. ***Esta camisa la** compré en Belk's* is **verbed** topicalization.

UNACCUSATIVE HYPOTHESIS: the discovery that the subject of many intransitive sentences is an underlying direct object. In terms of this proposal, the subject of many sentences is a **verbed**, because the sentence has no <u>verber</u> or its verber can be omitted.

UNDERGOER: *see* ACTOR and AGENT.

VERBED: the participant in a sentence that passes the **verbed** inference. It is the direct object of a sentence with a <u>verber</u> or the subject of a sentence. Without a <u>verber</u>. The secondary object of a double object sentence always passes the **verbed** inference.

VERBED INFERENCE: an inference that shows the postverbal participant in the unmarked word order in English and in Spanish of a transitive sentence (a sentence with <u>verber</u> and **verbed**). The only participant of a sentence without a <u>verber</u> passes the **verbed** inference (e.g. the only participant of a passive voice sentence).

VERBEE: the semantic role of the indirect object (or of the primary object). A role of verbee captures the generalization over recipient, goal, experiencer, beneficiary (benefactee), maleficiary (malefactee), possessor, source.

VERBER: the participant in a sentence that passes the <u>verber</u> inference. It is always the subject. In Spanish, it is the participant that agrees in person and number with the verb, if there is also a verbed.

VERBER INFERENCE: an inference that shows the preverbal participant in the unmarked word order in English and Spanish of a transitive sentence (a sentence with <u>verber</u> and **verbed**).

VERBERLESS: Many sentences can be verberless, but they are not subjectless: passive voice sentences; sentences with unaccusative verbs like *appeal*(1), *appear, belong, matter, occur, seem, sound*(1), etc.; sentences with a reflexive pronoun. If there is no <u>verber</u> in a sentence, the **verbed** is "promoted" to subject.

Index

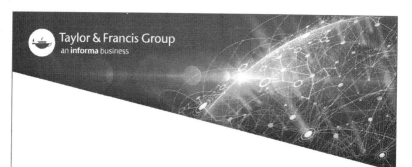